THE *New* Classroom Instruction THAT WORKS

ASCD MEMBER BOOK

Many ASCD members received this book as
a member benefit upon its initial release.

Learn more at www.ascd.org/memberbooks

THE *New* Classroom Instruction THAT WORKS

The Best Research-Based Strategies for Increasing Student Achievement

BRYAN GOODWIN
KRISTIN ROULEAU
with Cheryl Abla
Karen Baptiste
Tonia Gibson &
Michele Kimball

ascd | Arlington, Virginia USA

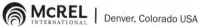
McREL INTERNATIONAL | Denver, Colorado USA

2800 Shirlington Road, Suite 1001 • Arlington, VA 22206 USA
Phone: 800-933-2723 or 703-578-9600 • Fax: 703-575-5400
Website: www.ascd.org • Email: member@ascd.org
Author guidelines: www.ascd.org/write

Penny Reinart, *Deputy Executive Director;* Genny Ostertag, *Managing Director, Book Acquisitions & Editing;* Mary Beth Nielsen, *Interim Director, Book Editing;* Susan Hills, *Senior Acquisitions Editor;* Katie Martin, *Editor;* Thomas Lytle, *Creative Director;* Donald Ely, *Art Director;* Lisa Hill, *Graphic Designer;* Circle Graphics, *Typesetter;* Kelly Marshall, *Production Manager;* Shajuan Martin, *E-Publishing Specialist*

Mid-continent Research for Education and Learning
4601 DTC Boulevard, Suite 500
Denver, CO 80237 USA
Phone: 303-337-0990 • Fax: 303-337-3005
Website: www.mcrel.org • Email: info@mcrel.org

First edition published 2001 as *Classroom Instruction That Works.* Second edition published 2012 under the same title. This publication (third edition) published 2023 as *The New Classroom Instruction That Works.*

ASCD® and ASCD LEARN. TEACH. LEAD.® are registered trademarks of ASCD. All other trademarks contained in this book are the property of, and reserved by, their respective owners, and are used for editorial and informational purposes only. No such use should be construed to imply sponsorship or endorsement of the book by the respective owners.

All web links in this book are correct as of the publication date below but may have become inactive or otherwise modified since that time. If you notice a deactivated or changed link, please e-mail books@ascd.org with the words "Link Update" in the subject line. In your message, please specify the web link, the book title, and the page number on which the link appears.

PAPERBACK ISBN: 978-1-4166-3161-3   ASCD product #122032
PDF EBOOK ISBN: 978-1-4166-3162-0; see Books in Print for other formats.
Quantity discounts: 10–49, 10%; 50+, 15%; 1,000+, special discounts (email programteam@ascd.org or call 800-933-2723, ext. 5773, or 703-575-5773). For desk copies, go to www.ascd.org/deskcopy.

ASCD Member Book No. FY23-2 (Nov. 2022 PSI+). ASCD Member Books mail to Premium (P), Select (S), and Institutional Plus (I+) members on this schedule: Jan, PSI+; Feb, P; Apr, PSI+; May, P; Jul, PSI+; Aug, P; Sep, PSI+; Nov, PSI+; Dec, P. For current details on membership, see www.ascd.org/membership.

Library of Congress Cataloging-in-Publication Data

Names: Goodwin, Bryan, author. | Marzano, Robert J. Classroom instruction that works.
Title: The new classroom instruction that works : the best research-based strategies for increasing student achievement / Bryan Goodwin, Kristin Rouleau, with Cheryl Abla, Karen Baptiste, Tonia Gibson, and Michele Kimball.
Description: Arlington, Virginia, USA : ASCD, [2022] | Includes bibliographical references and index.
Identifiers: LCCN 2022031950 (print) | LCCN 2022031951 (ebook) | ISBN 9781416631613 (Paperback) | ISBN 9781416631620 (pdf)
Subjects: LCSH: Effective teaching—United States. | Academic achievement—United States—Statistics.
Classification: LCC LB1025.3 .G6644 2022 (print) | LCC LB1025.3 (ebook) | DDC 371.102—dc23/eng/20220722
LC record available at https://lccn.loc.gov/2022031950
LC ebook record available at https://lccn.loc.gov/2022031951

32 31 30 29 28 27 26 25 24   4 5 6 7 8 9 10 11 12

THE *New* Classroom Instruction THAT WORKS

Bonus online-only content is available at www.ascd.org/TheNewCITW

Acknowledgments

While researching and writing this book, we remained humbly aware that we were standing on the shoulders of talented educators and researchers who created the first and second editions of *Classroom Instruction That Works*. Specifically, we'd like to acknowledge Robert Marzano, Debra Pickering, Jane Pollock, Ceri Dean, Bj Stone, Elizabeth Hubbell, and Howard Pitler. Their original vision of the need to translate best-available research into a manageable set of highly effective practices for teachers not only informed our efforts but also helped us envision what this edition could be. We thank them for blazing the trail for us.

We want to acknowledge our collaborators at McREL International, including researchers Chelsey Nardi and Paul Burkander, who helped to compile and vet the numerous studies that form the research base for this new edition of *Classroom Instruction That Works*. In addition, we owe a debt of gratitude to Roger Fiedler, Eric Hubler, and Ron Miletta, who provided invaluable editorial feedback and guidance from the manuscript's inception to completion.

We also wish to thank current and former members of the editorial team at ASCD, including Stefani Roth, who first made us realize that it was time for a new edition of the book, and Susan Hills and Katie Martin, for their keen editorial eye and constructive feedback throughout the production of this book. They helped us distill the best and most essential ideas from what was originally an expansive manuscript. Thank you for helping us to find, as Michelangelo put it, David in the marble.

In addition, we want to thank educators across many continents, regions, and cultures who applied what they learned from the first two editions and shared their experiences with us. A book like this one, no matter how thoughtfully or artfully crafted, is but a proverbial unheard tree falling in a forest until educators like yourselves pick it up and use it in professional practice. So, to all the educators out there we've interacted with since the publication of the first two books, thank you for your thoughtful questions, keen observations, and helpful advice. We hope we have done your feedback justice in our earnest attempts to ensure this book remains practical and useful.

Lastly, we are grateful to our families—parents, siblings, spouses, partners, and children—who encouraged us through the long process of writing a book during a pandemic, tolerating our incessant tapping away on laptops during evenings, weekends, and vacations. You were our sounding boards, and, of course, you remind us of what really matters the most—your love and support.

Introduction:
Professionalizing Education

Is teaching a profession? Most of us assume it is—after all, as educators, we spend countless hours in *professional* learning, and many of us accrue degrees and credentials to demonstrate our *professional* bona fides. But what exactly does it mean to be a professional? And can educators make the same claim to being members of a profession as, say, doctors, engineers, and lawyers?

We believe they can—and should.

After all, the heart of any profession is shared, precise knowledge—a common understanding of such things as human anatomy in medicine, the principles of building design in engineering, or prior case law and legal principles in jurisprudence. As we'll share in this book, teaching can (and should) be grounded in a robust body of scientific knowledge. In short, much like how doctors can diagnose a patient's illness and offer a prognosis, educators can draw upon science to discern student learning needs and use effective solutions to meet those needs.

The good news is these teaching solutions are neither secret nor beyond the reach of educators; you most likely already use many of them. However, educators often lack a shared understanding of evidence-based principles of effective teaching. The field resembles what Harvard researchers have described as "an occupation trying to be a profession without a practice" (City et al., 2009). That is, although research *should* inform classroom practice, teachers seldom have a shared understanding of this research, a common vocabulary for applying it, or a culture of working together to apply evidence to guide practice.

In contrast, other professions have well-developed professional understandings and vocabularies that allow, for example, doctors to work together to diagnose what may be ailing a patient or a large team of engineers to share design plans as they work to build a bridge. Although the science of teaching is somewhat newer than that of medicine or engineering, it is nonetheless a robust field—one that ought to establish teaching as not simply an art or trade-craft but a true profession. The core purpose of this book is to help teaching become a profession *with a practice* by moving beyond fads and unsubstantiated theories and drawing instead upon cognitive science and experimental studies.

Is a New Review of Research Really Needed?

This effort to synthesize recent research on teaching is the latest in a series of research projects at McREL International that started more than two decades ago, when a McREL team synthesized the best available research on instruction into a meta-analysis of research (Marzano, 1998). That analysis served as the basis for the book *Classroom Instruction That Works* (Marzano et al., 2001), which arguably transformed the landscape of education. Over the next decade, educators worldwide purchased more than a million copies of the book, and it was translated into more than a dozen languages. In the early 2010s, McREL embarked upon a two-year effort to update the meta-analysis (Beesley & Apthorp, 2010), resulting in a second edition of *Classroom Instruction That Works* (Dean et al., 2012).

Now, 20 years after the initial meta-analysis research and a decade after the second study and edition of the book, we believe it's time for another update. Over the past two decades, education research has evolved significantly, creating a growing collection of studies that employ scientific methods to measure, with far greater precision than ever before, the true impact of various teaching and learning strategies on student outcomes.

New Insights from a New Generation of Empirical Research

This new wave of research was prompted by a bipartisan federal push in the United States (and elsewhere in the world) for "gold standard" research in education, which helped to create a new science of teaching and learning. Although these newer studies reflect and reinforce much of what we found in our two previous studies, they also provide many new, compelling, and even surprising insights about what works in the classroom.

In simple terms, what most distinguishes this new generation of research studies is that they employ scientifically based research designs. This starts with randomly assigning students to (1) a treatment or experiment group that receives a particular intervention (e.g., a teaching or learning strategy) or

(2) a comparison or control group that typically receives business-as-usual instruction. Employing scientific design helps researchers ensure that findings are not simply the result of confounding variables such as students' level of poverty, prior knowledge, and ability—or teacher competence. This makes it easier to make causal claims (i.e., X causes Y) so that educators can be more certain of the effect of various teaching strategies on students.

Some Shortcomings of Earlier Research

Previous versions of *Classroom Instruction That Works* relied on best-available research, which at the time included studies that accomplished two very important tasks. First, these studies isolated a particular teaching strategy and, second, they quantified that strategy's effect on student outcomes. Although these studies were far more compelling than theoretical articles with at best anecdotal or qualitative evidence, many of them still did not reflect true scientific research. In fact, only about half—51 of 99—of the studies we examined for the second edition of the book could be classified as scientifically designed studies (Beesley & Apthorp, 2010).

As an example, in many of these studies, teachers and students were not randomly assigned to a treatment or control group. A group of students was chosen to receive a particular teaching approach, and researchers would then compare the performance of students in this group before and after the intervention with the performance of students in the general population. Such methodology can allow hidden factors to skew the findings. For example, if students receiving an intervention are already high performers poised for rapid growth in learning, the strategy might seem more effective than it is. Conversely, if students in the treatment group are hindered by more barriers to success than those in the general population, the strategy might seem less effective than it really is.

Many studies included in the original meta-analysis were also correlational. For example, they examined whether the amount of homework students reported doing each week was linked to their class grades (not surprisingly, it was). Yet correlation does not prove causation. Doing more homework *may* lead to better grades, but other factors could be at work. Students who report doing more homework might be more conscientious, more motivated, or more attentive in class. Or perhaps their parents are more likely to bug them about doing their homework or pressure them to get good grades. Increased hours of homework might simply reflect a press for achievement or motivation (however reluctant) among students to do their homework, get good grades, and keep their parents off their backs. In short, we cannot safely conclude from this correlation, however strong it might be, that teachers ought to pile more home-work on students.

Building on an Important Contribution to the Field

We understood all of this, of course, when we conducted our original meta-analyses. In fact, that's one of the main reasons we conducted a meta-analysis in the first place: we wanted to overcome the pitfalls of small sample sizes and potential confounding factors in previous studies. A meta-analysis essentially combines many smaller studies into a larger sample—much like media outlets do when they create "polls of polls" that merge smaller polls into larger polls in order to more accurately capture public sentiment with a smaller margin of error.

Similarly, in education research, combining several smaller studies (from which, individually, it might be difficult to draw strong conclusions) into a large sample lets researchers more confidently assert that certain teaching strat-egies support student learning. This is what made *Classroom Instruction That Works* so important and powerful: for many educators, it was the first time they had access to research-based, high-leverage strategies compiled into a single, easy-to-comprehend collection of teaching practices.

That said, meta-analyses have shortcomings. If not carefully constructed, they can, in effect, mix apples and oranges—force-fitting multiple studies into a single measure even though the studies may have examined several or slightly different approaches or strategies, such as different types of feedback (e.g., cor-rect answers or formative) or blended strategies (e.g., pairing cooperative learn-ing with problem-based learning). Meta-analyses may also obscure important subtleties. For example, some studies of feedback found *negative* effects on student learning, yet those negative effects vanished when examined in combi-nation with other studies reporting positive effects. Nonetheless, we might want to know *why* these differences emerged. Do certain types of feedback have less benefit for learning? Can feedback be less or more helpful in certain situations?

A New Approach for a New Generation of Research

With all this in mind, we took a different approach in developing the research base for this third edition—which we believe is sufficiently different to warrant the word "new" in the title. For starters, we applied review criteria from the Institute of Education Sciences' What Works Clearinghouse (WWC) to ensure the studies in our research base employed true scientific research designs and were peer-reviewed. Through this process, we identified 105 classroom-based studies that used scientific designs with sufficient sample sizes to offer valid causal claims about the effectiveness of the teaching strategies in question.

Moreover, in keeping with the idea that true scientific findings should be replicable across multiple studies, *The New Classroom Instruction That Works* highlights only strategies that have been found to be effective in seven or more studies. Typically, these strategies were examined across multiple grade levels, subject areas, and student populations, which suggests they are generalizable across all classrooms.

Also, this time we have chosen not to merge the quantitative results from these studies into a single effect size via a meta-analysis. As noted earlier, doing so can cloud important nuances in study findings and reflect a kind of psychometric sausage-making—pressing disparate studies together into something that, although more consumable, obfuscates important caveats, shortcomings, and insights from the original studies.

Instead of presenting a single effect size, we report how many studies support a particular strategy and list each of these studies with their respective effect sizes, using the WWC-prescribed measure of "improvement index" (see https://ies.ed.gov/ncee/wwc/glossary). This score provides the number of additional percentile points an average student (i.e., one at the 50th percentile) would gain after receiving the treatment intervention. For example, an improvement index score of 10 means that an average student in the treatment group would improve from the 50th to the 60th percentile after receiving the intervention (whereas an average student in the control group would remain at the 50th percentile).

That said, we remind readers that an effect size is simply an *estimate* of the impact of a particular strategy or set of strategies, not a guarantee. Studies of similar strategies, in fact, rarely report the same effect size (which illustrates the fact they are all estimates in the first place). When discrepancies in effect sizes arise in the rigorous studies we examined, we offer some explanation for why such differences might be present so that you, as a professional educator, can make your own judgments about how and when to use the practice in question with students.

Perhaps most important, our current review of research did not start with the foregone conclusion that the nine categories of effective teaching practices highlighted in previous editions of this text represented the final word on effective teaching strategies. Rather, like true scientists, we started from scratch, taking a fresh look at what a new generation of research tells us about effective teaching and which practices all teachers should build into their professional repertoire.

Focusing on Diversity, Equity, and Inclusion

Perhaps most important, in building the research base for this book, we intentionally searched for studies of interventions delivered to historically disadvantaged student groups, including students of color, students in poverty, emergent bilingual students, and those with low prior levels of achievement. As it turns out, a great deal of experimental research over the past two decades has explicitly focused on identifying effective interventions for these students. As a result, most of the 105 studies in our research base (see the Appendix) were conducted with diverse student populations. Specifically, we note the following:

- Fifty-five (52 percent) were conducted in classrooms where 40 percent or more of the population were students of color (African American, Hispanic, or Indigenous groups).
- Forty-five (43 percent) were conducted in classrooms where 40 percent or more of students qualified for free or reduced-price lunch.
- Thirty-four (32 percent) were conducted with students with an identified learning disability or identified as being at risk of academic failure due to low prior achievement.
- Twenty (19 percent) were conducted in classrooms where 25 percent or more of the student population were identified as emergent bilingual students.

The remainder of the studies included in our sample (30 studies—or 29 percent), were conducted in classrooms where the majority of students either did not reflect these student groups or demographic data were not reported. What this means is, instead of starting with research on general student populations and attempting to extrapolate findings to diverse learners, the research base for *The New Classroom Instruction That Works* starts with diverse learners and, thus, identifies teaching strategies proven to work for diverse learners. It's not surprising, then, that many of the strategies in this edition reflect what others have identified as "culturally relevant practices"—including making learning relevant to students, engaging them in critical thinking and reflection about their learning, and helping them to develop a positive view of themselves as learners through goal setting and peer-assisted learning. Perhaps most significantly, many of the teaching practices highlighted in this book were found to close learning gaps between historically marginalized student groups and their peers. Thus, the strategies highlighted here can help to define, in a scientific way, teaching practices that support more equitable outcomes for all learners.

New Guidance from New Research

As might be expected, our new methodology yielded a different set of high-leverage teaching strategies. Although many mirror those from previous editions, they differ in some important ways.

A smaller set of strategies

Most notably, we have identified a smaller set of strategies—winnowing down 48 strategies grouped under nine categories in the second edition of *Classroom Instruction That Works* to the 14 strategies in this book. This does not mean the strategies highlighted in previous editions *don't* work; it just means that in our new analysis, we were unable to find scientifically designed studies to support them. Nonetheless, as the saying goes, absence of evidence is not evidence of absence. In some cases, strategies identified through less scientific means (e.g., surveys or correlational studies) may still be valid. So, we do not advocate for teachers to abandon strategies highlighted in previous editions that have fallen off this list, especially if they find them beneficial. Rather, we would say this: the strategies highlighted in *The New Classroom Instruction That Works* have been shown, scientifically, to support better learning for diverse students.

Thus, we can unequivocally assert that teachers ought to master and include these strategies in their professional practice.

Practical guidance for each strategy

A strategy is only meaningful if teachers can readily apply it in their classrooms. Although this book is grounded in research, our intent is not to offer exacting details of each study but rather to "cut to the chase," so to speak, with practical guidance you can apply in your classroom. If you wish to dive more deeply into the research supporting each strategy, we provide tabular summaries in the Appendix and offer more detailed summaries of each study in a free online resource available at **www.ascd.org/TheNewCITW**.

We also recognize that what's most important with any evidence-based teaching strategy is how well teachers *adapt* it to the unique needs of their own learners. So, for each strategy, we highlight guiding principles that emerge from research and offer classroom tips for how you might apply these principles—not to prescribe one-size-fits-all approaches but to help you apply your own professional judgment in using these strategies to meet the unique needs of every learner in your classroom.

Links to the science of learning

We've linked these strategies with what is known about the science of learning as reported in our book, *Learning That Sticks* (Goodwin et al., 2020). In the two decades we've spent helping teachers apply the strategies in *Classroom Instruction That Works*, we have consistently found that the real inflection point in any teacher's professional growth (i.e., when they become true professionals) is when they become intentional in their use of evidence-based strategies (i.e., knowing not only *what* works but also *when* and *why* it works). Because the science of learning reflects how every human brain works regardless of cultural context or background, it offers insights that are valid for all students. Thus, we've aligned these strategies with the six phases of learning described in *Learning That Sticks* to illustrate how teachers can use them to, for example, help students "focus on new learning" or "make sense of learning."

The New Toolkit of Strategies

Our comprehensive review and analysis of scientific studies yielded 14 teaching strategies with significant positive effects for a diverse array of students.

Figure I.1 maps these strategies to the six phases of learning identified in *Learning That Sticks* (Goodwin et al., 2020).

FIGURE I.1   THE SIX PHASES OF LEARNING AND THE TEACHING STRATEGIES THAT SUPPORT THEM

LEARNING PHASE	TEACHING STRATEGIES
Become interested. To engage in learning, students must first become interested in and find content worthy of attention.	Strategy 1: Cognitive interest cues
Commit to learning. Because all learning requires sustained mental effort, students must commit to their learning.	Strategy 2: Student goal setting and monitoring
Focus on new learning. Once students are interested in and committed to learning, they must encounter it in ways that help them to master new knowledge and skills.	Strategy 3: Vocabulary instruction Strategy 4: Strategy instruction and modeling Strategy 5: Visualizations and concrete examples
Make sense of learning. All learning consists of connecting new knowledge with prior knowledge, aggregating ideas into manageable constructs or mental models, and integrating discrete skills into larger sequences that can be used to solve problems and accomplish tasks.	Strategy 6: High-level questions and student explanations Strategy 7: Guided initial application with formative feedback Strategy 8: Peer-assisted consolidation of learning
Practice and reflect. Once students have encountered and made sense of learning, they must retrieve and repeat it multiple times to store it in long-term memory.	Strategy 9: Retrieval practice (quizzing to remember) Strategy 10: Spaced, mixed independent practice Strategy 11: Targeted support (scaffolded practice)
Extend and apply. For students to store and retrieve new learning, they must engage with it in multiple ways—applying it to solve real-life, complex problems or extending it in novel ways.	Strategy 12: Cognitive writing Strategy 13: Guided investigations Strategy 14: Structured problem solving

We've organized the chapters of this book according to these six phases of learning. Each chapter offers a brief overview of the phase and the cognitive science behind it, then shares the teaching strategies aligned with that phase of learning. For each strategy, we offer guiding principles from research and practical tips for applying it in your classroom. The final chapter includes suggestions for working with your colleagues to embed these strategies into your own professional practice to ensure teaching becomes a profession *with* a practice in your school so that, together, you can support the success of every learner.

1

Helping Students Become Interested in Learning

At the risk of stating the obvious, to learn anything, one must pay attention to it—that is, become *interested* in it. As simple as that sounds, our brains are really good at ignoring what's going on around us. That's because, while our senses absorb an estimated 11 million bits of information per second, our brains can process only about 120 bits of that per second (Levitin, 2015). To avoid information overload, our brains disregard most of the stimuli in our environment and pay attention only to what we deem the most important bits of information.

The ramifications for teaching are considerable. Students' brains are designed to ignore most of what is going on in the classroom. It's on teachers, then, to use tried-and-true techniques—what we call *cognitive interest cues*—to help learning get past students' mental filters and into their brains. In this chapter, we'll share key findings and practical strategies from scientific studies that demonstrate the power of stimulating student interest as a critical precondition for learning.

What the Research Says

First, we'll explore why it's so important that students become interested in learning in the first place and what happens to student interest once they enter school. We'll also share an "open secret" to stimulating student interest that, sadly, remains untapped in many classrooms and schools.

Student engagement is as strongly correlated to student success as teacher quality

Here's the first big idea from research: *student interest and motivation matters.* Research shows that academic success is the result of many factors, including school and teacher quality, parental press for achievement, prior learning, and student interest and motivation. As it turns out, student interest and motivation have as much influence on academic success as teaching quality, long touted as the most important within-school factor linked to student success. Interest and motivation accounts for approximately 14 percent of the variance in student outcomes; teacher quality contributes to roughly 13 percent of the variance in their outcomes (Marzano, 2001).

In the real world, of course, student interest and motivation and teacher effectiveness are often intertwined; great teachers can and do spark student interest and motivation. Indeed, empirical research demonstrates that when teachers focus on sparking student interest, they can have significant positive effects on student motivation—and, in turn, on learning outcomes. This is particularly good news given that the same analysis of factors linked to student success (Marzano, 2001) found that student socioeconomic status accounts for 10 percent of the variance in their overall performance. In other words, a combination of motivated students and effective teachers can more than offset the barriers of socioeconomic status.

Student effort compensates for ability

A key reason interest and motivation are so strongly linked to student success is that motivation tends to translate into effort. Education research, in fact, confirms the old adage that "hard work beats talent when talent doesn't work hard." Using amount of time spent on homework as a proxy for effort, Keith (1982), for example, found that with just one to three hours of homework per week, so-called low-ability students (those at the 25th percentile on standardized aptitude tests) achieved grades commensurate with average-ability students (those at the 50th percentile) who spent no time on homework. Similarly, average-ability students who do two to three hours more homework per week than high-ability students (those at the 75th percentile or above) earn the same grades as high-ability students. In short, student ability is not a fixed trait; just 25 minutes per day of extra effort can lift students to higher levels of performance. Student effort matters a lot.

Students demonstrate less curiosity and engagement the longer they stay in school

Although student interest and motivation can contribute significantly to their performance, with each passing year in school, students become less motivated and engaged. A Gallup poll of 500,000 students from 5th to 12th grade, for example, found that while most (8 in 10) elementary students feel "engaged" in school—that is, attentive, curious, and optimistic about their learning—by high school, that number is halved (Busteed, 2013).

Certainly, teenagers expressing boredom and apathy is neither a new phenomenon nor a seismic shift in generational attitudes (who among us didn't complain of boredom while in school?). Nonetheless, we must ask ourselves why this happens. Why do so many middle and high school students complain of boredom when secondary school ought to be the very time they explore the mysteries of science, the complex drama of human history, the elegant language of math, and works of literature that reveal our shared humanity? Fortunately, student boredom need not be a fait accompli. Multiple studies point to practical ways teachers can spark student curiosity, interest, and motivation.

Internal rewards are more powerful motivators of deep learning than external rewards

Decades of psychology research suggests there are basically two ways to motivate students: (1) *external* rewards (e.g., using grades, gold stars, or stickers to bribe and cajole students into learning) and (2) *internal* rewards (e.g., helping them to find inherent interest and meaning in mastering new knowledge and skills). External rewards, sometimes referred to as "carrots and sticks," are commonplace in schools. Yet as Alfie Kohn (1999) observed, the net effect of using external rewards to motivate students is that, over time, students begin to see learning not as something they *want* to do but as a chore they *have* to do: something to be endured if they want candy, playground privileges, or a decent grade point average (GPA). For example, when researchers rewarded young children with cookies for drawing pictures (something they were doing for enjoyment prior to the study), those students became less likely to entertain themselves afterward by drawing pictures, presumably because the external rewards turned an erstwhile fun activity into something done to please others (Deci et al., 1999).

Teachers who rely on external rewards may send the wrong message: that learning is a trial to be endured rather that an opportunity to be relished and enjoyed. Moreover, 40 years of research show that extrinsic rewards only motivate performance on simpler tasks, whereas intrinsic rewards motivate performance on more complex tasks (Cerasoli et al., 2014). Some forms of learning, such as memorizing basic skills and facts, are simple and inherently less enjoyable for students. It's just good sense for teachers to occasionally use external rewards to motivate students to complete simple learning tasks, such as rewarding them with small prizes for beating their previous high score on multiplication tables. But if the goal is for students to engage in more complex learning—for example, to use basic math facts to solve complex, real-world problems—teachers need to help students identify the intrinsic rewards in learning by, for example, tapping into curiosity, personal experience, and interests. In Chapter 2 we'll explore different ways to encourage students to commit to learning.

Curiosity primes the brain for learning and supports retention of learning

Brain research shows that sparking curiosity not only makes learning more rewarding but also supports better retention of learning (Gruber et al., 2014). This, after all, is our true aim as educators: to ensure students both learn and remember the content they encounter in our classrooms. Basically, curiosity makes their brains thirsty for new learning and, thus, better able to retain learning. What this all adds up to is that student interest and motivation are essential to student success. Yet, as noted, the longer students stay in school, the less interest they experience in school.

Fortunately, empirical studies point to a tried-and-true strategy for motivating students by tapping into their curiosity, interests, and experiences: *cognitive interest cues.*

Strategy 1: Cognitive Interest Cues

Cognitive interest cues motivate learning by framing units and lessons in ways that make learning stimulating and relevant to students.

Experimental studies point to the power of sparking students' intellectual curiosity and making learning relevant to them, a strategy we call *cognitive interest cues.* We use the word *cognitive* intentionally here because the key is to get students thinking about what they will learn. Cognitive interest cues aren't simply gimmicks or classroom razzle-dazzle that grabs kids' attention but fails to prime their brains for learning. Rather, they are proven methods for helping students to become intellectually engaged and intrinsically motivated to learn. Collectively, these studies offer convincing evidence that teachers can (1) stimulate students' interest in learning and (2) in so doing, enhance student achievement.

We identified 14 studies with significant effects for which cognitive interest cues were a core element of the intervention (see the Appendix). These interventions had *improvement index* scores ranging from 8 to 49—which translates into raising the achievement of an average student (i.e., at the 50th percentile) from 8 to 49 percentile points. These studies have been conducted across multiple subject areas and grade levels, and with a diverse array of student populations. It's important to note that interest cues are seldom stand-alone strategies; more often, they are key elements of larger interventions, which suggests that this strategy should be integrated with other proven strategies.

Guiding principles for cognitive interest cues

The following guiding principles for cognitive interest cues emerge from these 14 studies.

Effective cognitive interest cues relate directly to desired learning outcomes.
You're likely familiar with presenters who open their remarks with a pithy anecdote or witty joke that might grab listeners' attention but has little connection to the topic at hand. Afterward, you might be able to recall the presenter's joke or anecdote . . . but not the actual content of their remarks. Teachers can make the same mistake in their classrooms. In an effort to grab students' attention, they share a funny video, tell an amusing anecdote, or make a reference to popular culture that has little to do with the learning at hand and may only serve to confuse students. So, it's important to note that, across all of the effective interventions studied, cognitive interest cues were carefully designed to draw students into the content at hand, anchoring their learning to curiosity-provoking questions or meaningful challenges.

For example, two studies (Bottge et al., 2014, 2015) found positive effects for "enhanced anchored instruction"—introducing students with learning difficulties to complex math problems with introductory videos designed to make problems interesting and relevant. One such video depicted three friends attempting to build a skateboard ramp on a budget, which required them to make measurements, convert feet to inches, calculate sales taxes, and solve other problems. Similarly, Vaughn and colleagues (2017) found positive effects for an intervention that included a "comprehension canopy" to frame social studies for 8th grade students in schools with high percentages of emergent bilingual students and students in poverty. At the start of each lesson, teachers engaged students in a 10- to 15-minute routine that included an engaging video clip framing the purpose for the upcoming lesson, linking new learning to prior knowledge, and cueing the thinking strategies students would need to apply during the lesson (e.g., comparison and contrast, cause and effect, perspective taking).

Hands-on learning experiences increase student interest.

Across multiple studies, cognitive interest cues engaged students in hands-on learning experiences designed to spark their curiosity and interest by translating abstract concepts into concrete puzzles, challenges, and problems to solve. For example, Guthrie and colleagues (2004) studied the effects of teaching science to a racially diverse group of 3rd graders with a combination of cognitive strategies (e.g., activating background knowledge, high-level questioning, graphic organizers, direct instruction of text structure) and motivational practices such as engaging students in hands-on learning experiences (e.g., dissecting owl pellets) and providing them with interesting texts to read related to their hands-on learning. Compared with a group receiving cognitive strategies alone and a control group receiving traditional instruction, the students who received both cognitive and motivational strategies significantly outperformed those receiving cognitive strategies alone (improvement index = 26) and those receiving traditional instruction alone (improvement index = 46).

Making personal connections to learning increases motivation and performance.

Experimental studies have also found that helping students draw personal connections to learning increases both their motivation and achievement. For example, Hulleman and colleagues (2010) found that college students who wrote short essays connecting what they were learning in a psychology course to their personal lives not only demonstrated greater interest in the course but also earned higher grades. Effects were even greater for students demonstrating low interest and achievement during the first half of the course.

Anand and Ross (1987) similarly demonstrated the benefits of helping racially diverse (52 percent African American) groups of students make personal connections to their learning, comparing the effects of engaging 5th and 6th grade students in three different versions of a computer-assisted lesson on division of fractions. In the first condition, personal information about the students (e.g., their friends, interests, hobbies) was incorporated into math problems. In the second condition, problems were presented with concrete (realistic but still hypothetical) contexts. In the third condition, problems were presented in a traditional abstract format. Afterward, students who received personalized problems not only reported greater interest in learning but also demonstrated higher performance on post-tests than students receiving problems with concrete representations only (improvement index = 31) and traditional problems with abstract representations (improvement index = 44).

Along similar lines, Cordova and Lepper (1996) found that students who engaged in a gamified version of math learning (i.e., solving math problems to "navigate a spaceship") with personal information (e.g., their own names, names of friends, favorite foods) embedded into the game demonstrated not only greater interest in learning but also better learning outcomes than students who engaged in a similar math game without the fantasy frame (improvement index = 49) or played the spaceship fantasy game without personal details included (improvement index = 37). In another study, a key component of an intervention for elementary school students with significant positive effects in improving student learning in social studies (improvement index = 49) and science (improvement index = 48) included a full day of concept lessons designed to cue cognitive interest by connecting academic concepts to racially diverse, low-income students' own lives (Dombek et al., 2017). Collectively, these studies demonstrate the power of helping students make personal connections to their learning.

Cognitively challenging learning increases student interest.

Multiple studies have demonstrated that low-achieving students don't need less rigorous or challenging lessons or texts. They actually benefit from the opposite—learning experiences that engage them in cognitively complex ideas and expose them to accessible yet thought-provoking texts. For example, in a large-scale study (Stevens, 2003) involving nearly 4,000 students in urban, high-poverty middle schools, the intervention was designed to engage students with high-interest, cognitively challenging texts from well-known authors (e.g., Langston Hughes, Pearl S. Buck, Isaac Asimov) and frequent, challenging writing exercises (e.g., "Write a short story in the style of O. Henry"). Students in the treatment group significantly outperformed those in the business-as-usual control group on measures of reading vocabulary (improvement index = 13), reading comprehension (improvement index = 10), and language expression (improvement index = 15).

Similarly, Kim and colleagues (2017) found positive effects for a yearlong approach to improving reading outcomes for a racially diverse (50 percent nonwhite) group of middle school students with a history of low levels of reading achievement (scoring at or below the 30th percentile) in schools with moderate to high levels of poverty (49–90 percent free and reduced-price lunch recipients). Students in the treatment group engaged in reading cognitively complex, personally relevant, and accessible fiction and nonfiction. In short, rather than simplifying or "dumbing down" learning in a misguided effort to make it more accessible, the intervention aimed to motivate students and cue cognitive interest by exposing them to readable texts that challenged their thinking and sparked their curiosity. Students who received the intervention demonstrated not only increased engagement in reading (improvement index = 31) but also statistically significant improvements in reading comprehension (improvement index = 8).

Classroom tips for cueing cognitive interest

Such studies demonstrate the power of stimulating student interest and curiosity by exposing students to cognitively challenging concepts and ideas, engaging them in hands-on and relevant learning, and helping them draw personal connections to their learning. Failing to stimulate student interest in learning is, in effect, asking them to overcome their own brains' natural mental filters in order to pay attention to what's happening in the classroom. On the other hand, stimulating students' interest in learning can make the entire process of learning more productive and joyful. Here are a few practical tips for translating this research into action in your classroom.

Activate prior learning to create a knowledge gap.
Activating prior knowledge is a powerful way to stimulate student interest (Guthrie et al., 2004; Vaughn et al., 2017). Curiosity itself is simply the recognition of a gap in knowledge, which requires a "reference point" (Loewenstein, 1994, p. 87). Students must know something about a topic before they can become interested in it. For example, you might be more apt to be curious about dog training if you've recently adopted a puppy.

In the classroom, it's important to help students connect new learning to prior knowledge by helping them see a critical gap in their knowledge; this creates a mental "itch" they want to scratch. Here's a straightforward template you can use as you begin to activate students' prior knowledge to stimulate their interest in new learning: "You know ____, but did/do you know ____?" For example:

- You know *how to calculate the area of shapes with straight sides,* but did you know *there's a "magic" formula you can use to calculate the area of a circle?*
- You know *about the ruins of an ancient civilization in the jungles of Central America,* but do you know *how this once mighty civilization disappeared?*
- You know *that people often make "slippery slope" arguments that predict that small actions will lead to disaster,* but did you know *such claims are actually logical fallacies?*

Questions are, of course, the heart of curiosity. As you plan a unit or lesson, consider first what prior learning students bring and second what new learning they will encounter. Doing so will help you to frame learning as a series of questions that help students activate their prior learning and connect it with what's coming next. See Figure 1.1 for some examples, organized by content area.

FIGURE 1.1   QUESTIONS THAT USE PRIOR LEARNING TO CUE COGNITIVE INTEREST

LANGUAGE ARTS	MATH	SCIENCE	SOCIAL SCIENCE	ARTS
You're all familiar with verbs. But did you know some verbs are weak and others are strong . . . and that good writers use strong verbs to "power up" their sentences?	You've likely heard mathematical predictions—for example, that a sports team has a 60 percent chance to win a game. But what does this really mean?	Based on what you've learned about the five animal groups, which do you think are best adapted to cold climates?	You've all used money to buy things. But have you ever wondered how does money *work?* Why do we accept a piece of paper in exchange for goods and services?	What did we learn from our color mixing that can help us create a one-color mosaic of different shades?
Have you ever finished reading something and realized you didn't absorb much of it? How can we read closely so this doesn't happen?	We've used linear equations to depict consistent proportional relationships. But what if relationships aren't consistently proportional?	You've all seen living things grow. What do you think may be going on deep inside them to make them grow?	Have you heard people criticize the president and other elected leaders? Did you know that in many nations such criticism is illegal? How did we get this right?	We've learned about the "rules" of minor chords and scales. What would it sound like if we "broke" those rules with additional chromatic notes called "blue notes"?

continued

FIGURE 1.1 QUESTIONS THAT USE PRIOR LEARNING TO CUE COGNITIVE INTEREST *(continued)*

LANGUAGE ARTS	MATH	SCIENCE	SOCIAL SCIENCE	ARTS
Have you noticed how people can view the same event quite differently? During this unit, we'll learn to appreciate how writers' different cultures and experiences influence their views.	How can we use what we've learned about mathematical modeling to predict the amount of water needed to support population growth in arid areas, like the Western United States?	If you've been near a beach in the summer, you've likely experienced daytime sea breezes and nighttime land breezes. What scientific principles might explain these phenomena?	We've seen how Rome struggled to maintain an empire spread across vast bodies of water and land and distinctly different cultures. What might be different for an empire, such as the Chinese, as they spread into more geographically and culturally cohesive regions?	Based upon what you've learned about modern dance in the United States, in what ways does it reflect the unique culture, heritage, and peoples of this country?

Use curiosity hooks.

Many of the effective interventions highlighted in this chapter began with teachers posing questions to hook student curiosity. There are some tried-and-true curiosity hooks that have emerged from research.

Mysteries. Robert Cialdini (2005), a psychologist at Arizona State University, wrote an article called "What's the Secret Device for Engaging Student Interest? The Answer Is in the Title." In it, he shared his epiphany after poring over dozens of science articles trying to figure out how to make complex content interesting for students. The best science writers, Cialdini noted, eschew the typical, yawn-inducing opener, "In this article, I will present arguments in favor of my theory of XYZ." Instead, they pose questions—questions like "What are the rings of Saturn made of—rock or ice?" Then they build suspense about their topic—arguments in favor of rock and of ice—before resolving the mystery. (The answer in this case is the rings of Saturn are made of both rock *and* ice.) You can take a similar approach in your classroom by presenting learning as a mystery. "What caused the wooly mammoth to go extinct?" "How could the vastly outnumbered American Colonial Army have defeated the British Empire?" "How do scientists measure the distance to faraway planets?" "What did people use before clocks were invented?"

Controversy. Research also shows that controversy begets curiosity (Loewenstein, 1994). In a now famous experiment, Lowry and Johnson (1981) randomly assigned 5th and 6th graders to work in groups. One group was instructed to come to a consensus about a particular topic (e.g., strip mining or designating wolves as endangered species); the other was encouraged to develop their own arguments regarding the topic. Students in the second group demonstrated more interest in the topic, sought more information on it, and were more likely to give up a recess period to watch a film about it.

Yes, some controversies may be too touchy to broach in classrooms (they might even be officially "off limits"), but many are not. Here are some examples:

- Are we victims of fate like the "star-crossed lovers" Romeo and Juliet, or do we have control over our circumstances?
- One way to reduce greenhouse gases would be to build nuclear power plants; after exploring the pros and cons of this energy source, what do you think?
- Is there another way to calculate the area of this irregular shape? Which is better and why?
- "Social media does young people more harm than good." How would you respond to this statement, using facts and logic to support your argument?

Riddles and suspense. Incomplete sequences (e.g., 1, 2, 3, 5, 8 . . . what comes next?), unfinished narratives (e.g., a cliff-hanger prior to a commercial break), and unsolved puzzles (e.g., $5 + x = 8$; $12 - x = 9$, what's x?) create suspense. Here are some examples of ways to create suspense in your classroom.

- We've seen that Ralph and Jack have very different personalities. They're both leaders, yet tension is brewing between them. What do you think will happen now that the boys are alone on the island?
- We know that mixing baking soda and vinegar together creates carbon dioxide. What will happen when we pour this mixture into a jar with a lit candle?
- We've seen complex alliances formed across Europe in the early 20th century. What might happen if a leader of one of these nations were assassinated?
- At what point does a square become a rectangle?

Cognitive conflict. Students also experience curiosity when they encounter something that conflicts with their prior learning or conceptions—for example, when they learn that winds blowing down from chilly mountaintops make the valleys below *warmer,* not colder, or that offering supermarket shoppers multiple flavors of jam makes them less likely to purchase a jar than when they were offered only a few choices. Cognitive conflict leaves students wondering, "Why *is* that?"

Students' common misconceptions are often a good way to create cognitive conflict. Here are some examples:

- When players make several shots in a row in a basketball game, do they really have a "hot hand" (like many people think), or does that streak of successful shots just reflect random, mathematical probability?
- A lot of students think the best way to study is to reread a chapter many times. As it turns out, that's not true. Today, we'll learn a better strategy.
- When a smaller nation encounters a larger one in a military conflict, does the larger nation always prevail? Not always!
- Which is cooler, the metal part of your chair or the fabric part? As it turns out, they're both the same temperature. The metal part of your chair feels cooler to the touch because of something we'll learn about today called "heat transfer."
- When you divide by a fraction, why do the numbers get larger?
- When you multiply a whole number by a decimal, the product is smaller than the original whole number. What happens when you divide using decimals?

A Hollywood axiom holds that a film that fails to hook audiences within the first 10 minutes is likely to bomb in theaters. The same might be said of classroom lessons and units. Like movie audiences, students bring varied interests, needs, motivations, and cultural lenses to the classroom. Some like mysteries, and others like solving problems and puzzles. Some students are motivated to help others, and some want to roll up their sleeves and engage in hands-on work. No single strategy is likely to fire every student's imagination, spark their curiosity, or make learning relevant to them. So, like a good movie, it's best to provide multiple "hooks" to draw students into learning. You can plan units and lessons to identify multiple ways to draw every student into learning (see the process outlined in Figure 1.2).

Help students make relevant connections to new learning.
Studies of both high school (Hulleman & Harackiewicz, 2009) and college students (Hulleman et al., 2010) have demonstrated that encouraging students to make personal and practical connections to new content improves both motivation and learning. Older students often can make connections with, for example, writing prompts that ask them to relate what they're learning to their own lives. Younger students may need additional support in making such

FIGURE 1.2   A PROCESS FOR PLANNING CURIOSITY HOOKS

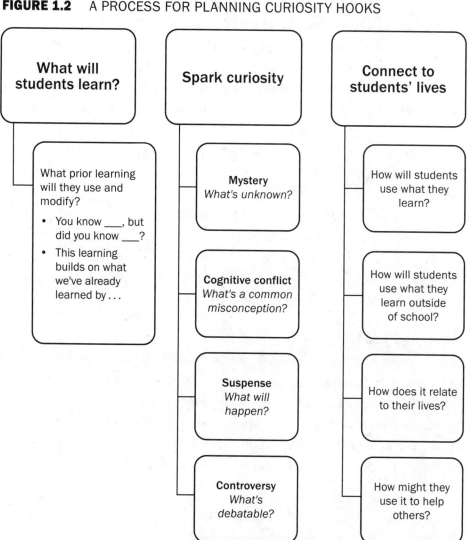

connections. A good way to begin is by showing them how to use what they are learning in the real world. Here are some examples:

- Adding, subtracting, multiplying, and dividing fractions is something we often must do. For example, if your recipe makes four servings but you need to bake for six, what do you do when the recipe says to use $1\frac{1}{2}$ cups of milk and $2\frac{1}{4}$ cups of flour?
- Have you ever seen something interesting and wanted to describe it to others? We are going to learn how writers and poets use words to paint pictures in other people's minds.

- I'm sure you hate feeling sick. During this unit we're going to learn what makes us sick and what's happening in our bodies when we're sick so that we can help our bodies fight the battle that rages inside them when we're sick and recover faster.
- Did you know most athletes use knowledge of angles to succeed in their sports? We are going to learn about angles and how they help athletes (and us) improve performance.
- Politicians are notorious for bending the truth in their speeches. We are going to learn how to identify false claims and replace them with credible facts and details.
- During the next few lessons, we will learn about gravity and centrifugal force, two forces that help you balance when you are riding a bike.
- Why is it important to be able to tell time on an analog clock? We are going to be able to read the clock at the back of the classroom so you can easily tell for yourself when recess, lunch, and specials are every day.

Get to know your students.

Because students bring different interests, motivations, and cultural lenses to your classroom, identifying hooks to stimulate their interests requires you to think beyond yourself and what *you* find interesting. Instead, take steps to identify which aspects of the content might resonate with your students. Simple writing prompts at the beginning of a semester or school year can help you learn more about your students' personal lives and interests:

- I often lose track of time when I'm _____.
- One thing I'm curious about right now is _____.
- If I could make one change in the world it would be _____.
- One interesting thing that most people don't know about me is _____.
- My family has instilled in me the value of _____.
- The person from history I would most like to meet is _____ because _____.
- I think the most important thing you should know about me as my teacher is _____.

The more you learn about your students, the more you can empower them to make their own connections to their learning. After all, it's more important that students find their *own* interests and reasons for learning than be told what to think or feel about their learning.

Final Thoughts: Disengaged Students ... or Disengaging Lessons?

We often hear teachers lament that their students are disengaged, as if disengagement were a personality trait or a character flaw. What the research demonstrates, however, is that student disengagement is a response to classroom conditions. Stated bluntly, *students disengage when classrooms are disengaging.*

In this chapter, we've reviewed some simple, straightforward strategies that you can use to pique student curiosity and hook their interest in learning. Yes, these strategies take some additional time to plan and deliver, but it's worth it. If your students don't pay attention to what's going on in your classroom—if they don't find it interesting, relevant, or meaningful—you can be assured they will not learn it.

Stimulating student interest is, of course, just the beginning of the learning process. Yet it can supercharge other effective teaching strategies and deliver tangible benefits for low-performing students. In Chapter 2, we'll explore the next phase of learning—which is, in effect, all about sustaining students' interest in learning by helping them to take ownership of their learning and steer it toward long-term memory.

2

Helping Students
Commit to Learning

Learning anything deeply requires sustained mental energy: paying attention to it, making sense of it, practicing it, and often re-encountering it until it becomes deeply embedded in long-term memory. In short, learning requires our brains to stay powered up for long periods of time. Yet as cognitive scientist Daniel Kahneman notes, "One of [the brain's] main characteristics is laziness, a reluctance to invest more effort than is strictly necessary" (2011, p. 31). This means that, to learn anything, we must convince our brains that it is worth the effort to remain powered up and focused on learning. And doing that requires a commitment to learning, the second of the six phases of learning.

In this chapter, we'll explore some key insights from cognitive science and important findings from experimental research that point to a practical strategy to help students commit to learning.

What the Research Says

We'll start with what cognitive science tells us about why it's often difficult for students to commit to learning, which explains the importance of helping tap into powerful chemicals in their brains they need to stay "powered on."

Learning requires tremendous mental energy

The process of learning requires something Kahneman calls "effortful thinking" (2011, p. 40). As he explains it, the brain has two operating systems. One is the *fast-thinking* brain, which operates automatically, with little thought, often because it reactivates prior learning that's been converted into automated mental scripts. For example, once you learned to ride a bike, your fast-thinking brain took over, letting you cruise down the street without giving much thought to staying balanced, steering, or pedaling. The second system is the *slow-thinking* brain, which requires focused attention. For example, when first learning to ride a bike, you needed to focus all of your attention on the mechanics of pedaling, steering straight, and maintaining your balance. The slow-thinking brain can easily get interrupted when attention is diverted—for example, when a novice bike rider attempts to wave at a camera and promptly veers off into the curb. Generally speaking, the slow-thinking brain is in charge (it is akin to stream of consciousness). Yet, as Kahneman notes, the brain constantly wants to slide back into low-energy mode and avoid learning and other forms of effortful thinking, especially if there isn't any reward in that effort. This leads us to the next big idea.

Setting and achieving goals makes learning more rewarding

Fortunately, some forms of thinking can be sufficiently rewarding to convince our brains to stay powered up. Satisfying curiosity fills the brain with the "reward molecule" dopamine (Gruber et al., 2014). The same goes for achieving a goal; even something as simple as checking an item off a to-do list delivers a dopamine reward. In short, achieving a goal feels good and creates a positive addiction—one that can be powerful enough to convince the brain that all of that effortful thinking was worth it for the dopamine reward at the end.

Goals are, of course, more meaningful when we set them for ourselves, rather than have them handed to us. For example, most people would resent someone else giving them (or even suggesting) a New Year's resolution. Yet that is, in effect, what a teacher does when presenting learning goals to students without inviting their ownership of those goals. To truly help students commit to learning, teachers need to help students set personal goals so that they can see what they are learning as valuable and achievable.

Students are more likely to pursue goals they find meaningful and achievable

Researcher Jere Brophy (2004) consolidates 25 years of research on student motivation into a simple formula: *value × expectancy*. You can help students address the first of half of this equation—*value*—using cognitive interest cues that convince their brains they *want* to learn something (e.g., because it's fascinating), *need* to learn something (e.g., because it's useful) or feel they *should* learn something (e.g., because it will help someone else). You can address the second half of this equation—*expectancy*—by helping students break larger goals into smaller steps that create a path to success. For example, in a study conducted years ago, Bandura and Schunk (1981) found that students who set realistic, short-term personal goals (e.g., completing six pages of instructional materials per class session) had greater success than those who set "distal" learning goals (e.g., aspiring to complete all 42 pages over seven sessions) or no goals at all.

Mastery goals are more powerful than performance goals

For goals to truly help students to commit to learning, they ought to be framed as goals for *learning,* not simply achieving a grade. In a series of classroom experiments, Stanford University researcher Carol Dweck and her colleagues (2000) demonstrated that students who set performance goals for learning—goals that reflect wanting to "look smart . . . and avoid looking dumb" (e.g., "I want an *A* in my English class")—were more likely to feel helpless, inadequate, and frustrated in the face of learning challenges. On the other hand, students who set mastery goals that reflected an innate "desire to learn new skills, master new tasks, or understand new things—a desire to get smarter" (e.g., "I want to become a better writer") were more likely to take initial failures in stride and press on to accomplish their goals (Dweck, 2000, p. 15).

Students are more apt to commit to learning when they connect effort with success

It's also important to teach students—often directly—the link between effort and success. Psychologist Martin Seligman spent his career studying why some people are more successful than others. He found that successful people tend to chalk up their successes (and failures) to their own efforts (or lack thereof) versus luck or misfortune—a trait he called "learned optimism," as opposed to "learned helplessness" (2006, p. 15). Learned optimism, Seligman noted, often emerges through "mastery experiences"—opportunities to experience success, including accomplishing small goals. Over time, as students set and achieve goals, they see their successes not as the result of luck or talent but rather their own efforts and are thus more apt to see themselves as masters of their own destinies.

This single factor, called *fate control*, has a more powerful positive (or negative) influence on student achievement than any other factor within a school's control (Coleman, 1966). Over the past few decades, in fact, researchers have found that whether students have an *internal* locus of control (i.e., they believe they can shape their life outcomes through their own actions) versus an *external* locus of control (i.e., they see their circumstances shaped by external forces beyond their control) is one of the strongest predictors of success in school and life. For example, high school dropouts are more apt to have an external locus of control (Ekstrom et al., 1986), whereas high-achieving, low-income, nonwhite students are more likely to have an internal locus of control (Finn & Rock, 1997).

For marginalized students, a strong internal locus of control can counteract the detrimental effects of "stereotype threat," the well-documented phenomenon of students performing poorly when they feel at risk of being judged on the basis of their race, gender, or other social identity. Richardson and colleagues (2012) found that feeling in control over one's life, academic self-efficacy, and goal orientation contributed to roughly 20 percent of the variance in university students' GPAs. This is nearly the same predictive power as high school grades and entrance exam scores.

Strategy 2: Student Goal Setting and Monitoring

Engaging students in goal setting and monitoring helps them remain committed to learning.

Although the brain prefers to avoid the effortful thinking required for learning, research shows that goal setting is a powerful way to overcome this natural tendency to revert to low-effort mode. When you help students set and achieve personal goals for learning, you are helping them train their brains to expect dopamine rewards from effortful thinking and, thus, remain committed to learning. Perhaps the best news of all, though, is that by giving students ongoing opportunities to set and achieve learning goals, teachers can help them see that effort is the key to success. Goal setting helps to foster an internal locus of control that supports lasting success in school and life. In light of all this, it's not surprising that empirical research points to a single, powerful classroom strategy for helping students commit to learning: *student goal setting and monitoring.*

We found 16 empirical studies that have demonstrated significant effect sizes (improvement index = 14–47) for interventions that incorporate student goal setting (see the Appendix). Positive effects were found across all subject areas, grade levels, and student populations. In most studies, student goal setting was bundled with other teaching strategies, which stands to reason. After all, goals are necessary but not sufficient for learning—students still require effective learning experiences to achieve their goals. Nonetheless, a few researchers have isolated the power of learning goals and found that encouraging students to set goals for learning has a powerful effect on learning outcomes.

Guiding principles for student goal setting and monitoring

The following key principles for student goal setting and monitoring emerge from these studies.

Concrete, achievable goals are highly effective for straightforward tasks.

Goals need not be incredibly ambitious to be effective—especially when the learning at hand is relatively straightforward. In fact, students perform better on less complex tasks (e.g., memorizing math facts, revising essays) that have clear and achievable goals (e.g., beating their own previous records for correct answers, adding a specified number of details to support their writing; Fuchs et al., 1997, 2003; Page-Voth & Graham, 1999). As we've seen from brain research, achieving straightforward goals can provide students with sufficient bursts of dopamine to make learning rewarding and help students stay committed to learning.

Specific learning goals are better than vague ones.

Studies comparing the effects of students setting specific goals versus imprecise ones (e.g., "do your best") have consistently demonstrated strong effects for specific goals and weak effects for vague ones (e.g., Graham et al., 1995; Midgette et al., 2008; Schunk & Swartz, 1993). For example, Schunk and Swartz (1993) compared the writing performance of 40 mostly Black and Hispanic 4th grade students who received similar writing instruction but with four different goal-setting conditions:

- The first group focused on *process* goals, for example, to learn how to use certain steps to write a descriptive paragraph.
- The second group focused on the same process goals, but also received progress feedback three to four times per lesson.

- The third group focused on *product* goals, for example, setting a goal to write a descriptive paragraph.
- The fourth (control) group set vague "try to do your best" goals.

Despite initially demonstrating similar writing abilities, six weeks after the intervention, students who set process goals and received feedback scored significantly higher on a test of writing skills than those with process goals alone (improvement index = 33), product goals (improvement index = 40), or vague goals (improvement index = 50).

Goals are more effective when paired with feedback.

Several studies have demonstrated the power of pairing goal setting and progress feedback or progress monitoring (Fuchs et al., 1997, 2003; Glaser & Brunstein, 2007; Limpo & Alves, 2014; Schunk & Swartz, 1991). For example, Fuchs and colleagues (2003) compared the effects of integrating goal setting and self-evaluation with schema-based instruction (i.e., teaching students to transfer math solution methods across different problems) versus schema-based instruction alone. Their study included racially diverse (>60 percent nonwhite) and low-income (>60 percent receiving free or reduced-price lunch) students, as well as those with identified learning disabilities (>67 percent). Students in the first treatment group set goals to beat their own previous high scores or achieve perfect scores and used an answer key to evaluate their work and chart daily progress. Students in the second treatment group engaged in only schema-based instruction without goal setting or self-evaluation, and a control group received conventional classroom instruction without goal setting. Students in the goal-setting-plus-self-evaluation group significantly outperformed those in the schema-based-instruction-only group on immediate and delayed measures of their ability to transfer problem-solving methods across problems (improvement index = 17 and 22, respectively).

Students should set mastery (not performance) goals.

Many studies have demonstrated the positive effects of encouraging students to set mastery goals instead of performance goals (e.g., Glaser & Brunstein, 2007; Graham et al., 1995; Guthrie et al., 2004; Limpo & Alves, 2014; Midgette et al., 2008; Morisano et al., 2010; Schunk & Swartz, 1993). For example, Midgette and colleagues (2008) randomly assigned 5th and 8th grade students to three different types of goal-setting strategies for revising first drafts of a persuasive essay. The first group was given a vague goal to "make any changes that you think would improve the essay." The second was encouraged to attain a more specific content goal, to "add more reasons and evidence" to their essays. The third was encouraged to achieve a broader mastery goal—namely, to consider who might disagree with their opinion and to develop counterarguments in response. Students in this third group wrote significantly more persuasive final essays than those in the content goal group (improvement index = 19), who in turn outperformed students in the general goal group (improvement index = 18). These findings point to the power of helping students set goals that focus on the larger purpose of their learning—in this case, to persuade skeptical readers—as opposed to simply writing a good essay or supplementing their writing with details.

Students with a growth mindset are more likely to exert effort to achieve goals.

Perhaps most important, setting and achieving mastery goals can support what Carol Dweck's decades of research have identified as a powerful predictor of student success: the extent to which they adopt a "growth mindset" as opposed to a "fixed mindset" (Dweck, 2006). Students who adopt a growth mindset see achievement or success as the result of effort, not talent, and are thus more likely to exert effort to achieve goals. They understand that, like a muscle, the brain grows stronger with use and that learning requires effort, practice, and relearning. Conversely, students with a fixed mindset see achievement or success as something innate, not earned nor developed through effort. As a result, they tend to feel helpless in the face of challenges or setbacks, view feedback as criticism, and ultimately learn less and demonstrate less success as learners.

In a controlled classroom experiment, Blackwell and colleagues (2007) demonstrated the power of teaching students to develop a growth mindset when setting goals. Through a series of 25-minute lessons, researchers taught a randomly selected group of 7th graders—mostly students of color (52 percent African American, 45 percent Hispanic) who were previously low achieving in mathematics—that they could grow their intelligence and abilities through effort. Class readings, discussions, and activities impressed upon students that, like muscles, brains grow stronger with frequent use, and they could control this as learners. By the end of the semester, students in the treatment group not only exhibited greater growth mindset but also reversed previous declines in their math grades, achieving significantly higher grades (improvement index = 20) than students in the control group, who spent the eight sessions learning about the science of memory.

Classroom tips for student goal setting

Goals challenge students. They also challenge teachers to be clear about *what* exactly they want students to learn and *why*. The interventions examined in most of these studies were, in fact, specific, short-term goals focused on what students would learn in a limited period of time. In some cases, student goals were more long term, such as setting a mastery goal for a class or unit of study or envisioning a desired future state and setting life goals (Morisano et al., 2010).

Both short- and long-term goals are powerful. Recalling Brophy's (2004) formula for motivation (*expectancy × value*), short-term goals can support student expectancy by helping students to break down learning into achievable, bite-sized chunks. Long-term goals, especially those tied to mastery, can help students see value in what they're learning. Of course, helping students set compelling personal long-term goals for learning requires that you are clear on not only what you want students to learn but why you are asking them to learn it.

In *Learning That Sticks* (Goodwin et al., 2020), we suggest teachers borrow a page from Madison Avenue advertising executives and identify the WIIFM ("What's in it for me?") for students. The more you can help students connect their learning goals to mastering useful knowledge and skills, pursuing their interests, or satisfying their curiosity, the more you can help them remain committed to learning. With all of this in mind, we offer these practical tips for helping your students commit to learning with challenging, achievable, and meaningful learning goals.

Explicitly teach goal setting and help students internalize why it matters.

Collectively, the studies highlighted in this chapter demonstrate that few students naturally stumble on the practice of setting goals. Instead, you must teach the process to them and help them to appreciate the power of goal setting in their own lives. One way to do this—especially for students who may initially lack internal locus of control—is to help them set short-term, realistic, and measurable goals that provide opportunities to connect effort with success. Another way is to encourage students to share the power of goal setting with other students who may want to give up or feel unwelcome at school.

An experiment involving Black and white first-year college students (Walton & Cohen, 2011) further demonstrated the benefits of teaching goal orientation to diverse student populations. Participants in the treatment group read materials stating that all students, regardless of race or background, experience temporary setbacks and feelings of self-doubt during their first year of college. They were then asked to relate their own experience to what they had read and create a message for other students to reassure them that doubts about belonging in college were normal and setbacks temporary. Although this intervention had no effect for white students, it boosted the GPAs of Black students so much it eventually cut the achievement gap by 79 percent and tripled the number of Black students in the top quarter of their class. The key to these positive results appears to be the "saying-is-believing" effect (Walton & Cohen, 2011, p. 1448). In short, sharing the benefits of persisting toward goals with others helped students internalize these attitudes within themselves.

Ensure goals and learning objectives are specific.

As we've seen, vague goals and learning objectives have little, if any, effect on student learning. The clearer goals and learning objectives are for students, the easier it is for them to commit to learning; they know exactly what's expected of them and what success looks like each step of the way. For most students, especially younger students or those who are struggling, breaking learning into bite-sized bits that describe success (while still ensuring they keep the bigger picture in mind) can be particularly helpful. As Schunk and Swartz's study (1993) demonstrates, if students are learning a process for writing a descriptive paragraph, their goals should help them focus not on simply writing *a* paragraph, but on mastering the process of writing effective paragraphs. Here's an illustration to clarify the hierarchy of goals, learning objectives, and success criteria:

- **Long-term goal:** We will become skillful at writing opinion essays using data and relevant details so that we can effectively communicate our ideas in writing.
- **Unit learning objective:** We will write an opinion essay that includes supporting details from credible sources in order to persuade others to share our opinion.
- **Success criteria:**
  - I can analyze the strengths and weaknesses of opinion essays as I learn to write my own effective opinion essay.
  - I can explain how I know that the details I selected are credible.
  - I can discuss with a partner the difference between persuading and informing.

In addition to long-term goals and unit-learning objectives, students can also set daily learning objectives or success criteria (see Figure 2.1).

FIGURE 2.1   DAILY LEARNING OBJECTIVES AND RELATED
STUDENT GOALS

DAILY LEARNING OBJECTIVE	STUDENT LEARNING GOAL (SUCCESS CRITERIA)
Vague: We will write an opinion essay. *Specific:* We will use a graphic organizer to plan an opinion essay that includes a topic and supporting details **so that** we have the necessary information to begin writing. We will give and receive feedback about our essay plans **so that** we don't have gaps in our information.	I can use the text to identify a topic (and my opinion) for my essay. *Example:* I believe the most influential character in the story was _____. I can identify three relevant details from the text that support my topic and opinion. I can discuss my opinion and supporting details with a partner and add information if necessary. I can use a feedback protocol to give my partner specific feedback about their work.
Vague: We will use the text to add more details to our opinion essays. *Specific:* We will use the text to add statements of explanation to our relevant details **so that** it is clear how the text supports each detail and gives credibility to our opinion.	I can write two statements of explanation for each of my details. *Example:* This detail about Grandma explains her relationship with other family members: they saw her as having wisdom, which made her very influential. I can explain to a partner exactly where I found information in the text to support my explanations.
Vague: We will write conclusions for our essays. *Specific:* We will learn about what makes a conclusion effective **so that** we can write a strong concluding statement.	I can analyze two opinion essays with my group and add to the class chart outlining the characteristics of their conclusions. *Example:* Effective conclusions restate the opinion and very briefly summarize the evidence supporting the opinion. I can analyze a third conclusion on my own, applying the information we generated as a class. I can draft a conclusion statement and highlight how I have incorporated characteristics of effective conclusions in my work.

Notice how the student learning goals in Figure 2.1 translate vague objectives into more meaningful goals for students by providing the *how* to support the *what* and *why* of the specific learning objective. When students know what they will learn (what makes a conclusion effective), why they're learning it (so that we can write a strong concluding statement), and how they will engage in learning and monitoring their progress (analyze two opinion essays with my group and add to the class chart outlining the characteristics of effective conclusions), it provides a clear pathway and motivation for learning.

Use first-person stems to help students personalize objectives as success criteria.

Simply posting a learning objective in the front of a classroom does little to improve learning if students do not translate the objectives into personal goals for learning. In our visits to classrooms, we often see learning objectives framed as goals for *teaching* (e.g., "Today's lesson will focus on . . ."). A key breakthrough for many teachers, however, is when they begin phrasing learning objectives to describe what *students* will *learn* and why ("Today we will learn . . . so that we can . . ."). Success criteria sentence stems include phrases such as the following:

- I can explain . . .
- I can illustrate and explain . . .
- I understand and can discuss . . .
- I can test and prove . . .
- I can demonstrate how to . . .

Being able to use such verbs as "explain," "describe," or "predict" helps students focus on mastery, not simply on performance goals. Figure 2.2 shows a rubric that translates a learning objective into a number of success criteria (student learning goals). Students might use a tool like this to both monitor their progress and build familiarity with the idea that within each objective are specific goals for them to master.

Help students monitor progress toward their goals and objectives.

Several studies have demonstrated the benefits of pairing goal setting with self-monitoring and regular progress feedback. Goals are supposed to help students not just commit to learning but stay committed to learning. Here are a few simple strategies we've seen teachers use to help students keep their goals in front of them (sometimes literally) and use them to monitor progress:

- Invite students to write their learning goals on table cards placed in front of them.
- Invite students to write weekly learning goals on the reverse side of their student ID placards.
- Encourage students to evaluate their own progress using checklists, rubrics, or entries in e-portfolios.
- Use graphs or charts to help students track daily or weekly progress toward their goals.
- As a bell-ringer activity, invite students to revisit their goals, reflect on their progress, and set new goals as needed.

FIGURE 2.2   A STUDENT RUBRIC REFRAMING A LEARNING OBJECTIVE AS A SERIES OF SUCCESS CRITERIA

Learning objective: We will learn to write opinion essays so that we can express our ideas more clearly to others.			
I can explain the difference between an opinion and a fact.	😐	🙂	🥰
I can tell a classmate my opinion about a topic.	😐	🙂	🥰
I can include a personal example and two reasons to support my opinion.	😐	🙂	🥰
I can write my opinion, personal example, and two reasons in three to five sentences in complete thoughts.	😐	🙂	🥰

- Use "turn and talk" to encourage students to share and discuss their learning goals with a peer.
- Have students create a weekly or biweekly voice recording or video diary explaining progress toward their goals.

Help students develop mastery goals.

As we've noted, sometimes simple goals tied to performance can be effective—for example, encouraging students to beat a prior score on a weekly quiz. Ultimately, though, it's vital that students develop a growth mindset about their goals—seeing them as opportunities to challenge themselves to exercise their brains and become stronger learners. So, although performance goals can be helpful in the short-term, it's important to help students set learning goals that are about mastering new learning and not simply achieving a desired score or grade. Figure 2.3 (see p. 38) provides some examples of how performance goals can be reframed as mastery goals.

FIGURE 2.3   PERFORMANCE GOALS REFRAMED AS MASTERY GOALS

PERFORMANCE GOAL	MASTERY GOAL
I'll get an *A* on my persuasive essay.	I'll master the six elements of persuasive writing.
I'll pass my Earth Science test.	I'll be able to understand and explain how the mountain range near my home formed and changed over time.
I'll get a perfect score on the math quiz.	I'll practice and master the skills I need to measure irregular shapes.
I will get 10/10 on my spelling test.	I will be able to use "their," "they're," and "there" correctly in sentences.
I will memorize the periodic table.	I will be able to discuss the elements in the periodic table and explain why it's structured the way it is.
I will learn all of my shapes.	I will be able to explain the attributes of each shape.
I will learn all of the letters.	I will be able to classify upper and lowercase letters.
I will create a plant cell.	I will create a plant cell and teach my classmates the process of photosynthesis using the correct academic vocabulary.

Final Thoughts: Helping Students Develop Positive Habits of Mind

When students set goals, they learn more. Having goals for learning activates metacognitive strategies. *Metacognition* is self-talk—the voice in students' minds that helps them stay committed to learning by reminding them to stay focused, pointing out when they're off-track, and encouraging them to keep exerting mental effort to reach their goals. Another study in our sample illustrates this power of goals to support positive self-talk and commitment to learning—not just over a single class period or unit, but over an entire semester or longer.

Morisano and colleagues (2010) randomly selected a group of academically struggling university students (GPA of 3.0 or less) to engage in a relatively brief (2.5-hour) web-based, intensive goal-setting program that guided them through a series of steps to visualize their ideal future, identify areas of interest they wanted to learn more about, set specific goals to realize their desired state, identify steps to take to achieve their goals, and clarify their commitment to each goal. Meanwhile, a control group of similarly struggling college students took a series of psychology surveys and wrote about positive past experiences. After four months, participants in the goal-setting group achieved significant improvements, with GPAs rising from 2.25 to 2.91 on average, whereas students in the control group demonstrated no significant changes in achievement.

What this study and others in this chapter illustrate is that helping students set goals for learning is more than a simple classroom teaching strategy—it's a powerful habit of mind. Setting goals creates a positive feedback loop: the more challenging the goal, the more dopamine our brains release when we achieve it, thus encouraging us to set and measure progress on ever more challenging goals. Goal setting, especially when combined with cognitive interest cues, makes learning rewarding (and perhaps even addictive), prompting students to commit to learning not because they *have* to, but because they *want* to. And that makes the whole learning experience more joyful and engaging for everyone—students and teachers alike.

3

Helping Students
Focus on New Learning

Once students' brains are primed to learn, they're ready to engage in the third of the six phases of learning: focusing on new learning.

Typically, "new learning"—information that's stored in what cognitive scientists refer to as "short-term working memory"—is retained for only 5 to 20 minutes. It's a bit like an open window on your computer screen; you have no trouble focusing on what you see before you, but you might lose the information forever if you close the window. What's in working memory can go just one of two places: either it leaves (i.e., you forget about it, like when you go to another room to fetch something only to find that you have forgotten why you've come) or it begins the journey to long-term memory. As a teacher, your goal is to help students focus on new learning sufficiently to ensure it makes its way into long-term memory.

In this chapter, we'll explore some key insights from cognitive science and important findings from experimental research that support three practical strategies for helping students focus on new learning.

What the Research Says

There are some "big ideas" about short-term working memory, which, as it turns out, explain why the three strategies we highlight are so effective.

Short-term working memories have limitations

Your short-term working memory can only focus on a handful of information at once. Out of the 11 million bits per second streaming in through your five senses, your brain can only process about 120 bits per second (Levitin, 2015). Understanding someone speaking to you, for example, requires about 60 bits per second, which explains why it's difficult to comprehend two people talking at the same time and impossible to follow three conversations at once. You simply cannot squeeze 180 bits of information into a 120-bit pipe. In addition, working memory's overall capacity is limited. Long thought capable of juggling just seven plus or minus two bits of information (Miller, 1956), working memory's "information bit limit" may actually be closer to four (University of New South Wales, 2012). In practice, our brains tend to cluster longer strings of information into shorter ones. For example, unless you're familiar with a certain '80s pop song, you're more likely to remember "867-5309" if you translate it into "8, 67, 53, 09."

Working memories focus better on new information presented visually and verbally

Fortunately, even though our working memories can only process limited amounts of data at once, we can, in effect, double our information processing abilities if we receive information both visually and verbally—something referred to as "dual coding" (Paivio, 1991). Studies show that when we simultaneously activate the visual and verbal systems of our working memories, we are better able to process and store new information. So, it's not surprising that pairing visual with verbal information through the use of visualizations and concrete examples is a powerful teaching strategy.

Automating key processes and skills helps to reduce cognitive demand on working memory

Our brains also overcome the limited bandwidth of working memory by turning complex mental processes into automated scripts, akin to a macro in a computer program. Right now, as you read this sentence, without being consciously aware of it, your brain is automatically translating the letters of each word in this sentence into sounds, syllables, and words so you can focus on comprehending the meaning. It's a nifty trick—one your brain does so effortlessly it can be easy to forget the painstaking learning and practice that allowed you to automate the mental scripts you now employ so effortlessly—which brings us to another key idea.

Direct instruction helps students learn processes and skills more easily and efficiently

This whole process of automation is made easier and more efficient through initial direct instruction and demonstration of new processes and skills. Yes, the brain can (and does) automate skills through self-discovery and trial and error, but that's inefficient and leaves too much room for error and learning falling through the cracks. In short, you should not assume students will naturally discover on their own how to read, add numbers, comprehend text, solve word problems, or write effectively. Rather, you must help them develop these skills by explicitly teaching and modeling the steps required to do these things well. This is the key idea behind another evidence-based teaching strategy, strategy instruction and modeling (see Strategy 4, p. 50).

Using subject-specific and academic vocabulary supports deeper learning

Another way our brains take the burden off our working memories is by compressing ideas and concepts into mini packets of knowledge called "words." For example, when you fully understand the meaning of "condensation," your brain associates this word with concepts (e.g., water phasing from vapor to liquid) and visual images (e.g., moisture on a cold glass). This is the key idea behind vocabulary instruction—helping students to translate big ideas and concepts into those manageable packets of information we call words. It is much easier, for example, to understand a complex concept like the water cycle if you understand the word "condensation."

In this chapter, we'll explore how to translate these guiding principles into classroom strategies that help your students effectively focus on new learning while it's in their working memories.

Strategy 3: Vocabulary Instruction

Vocabulary instruction builds declarative knowledge by helping students understand, recall, and apply subject-specific words and academic terms.

Vocabulary development has long been linked to student success and reading comprehension (Beck et al., 1982), likely because, as Henry Ward Beecher famously wrote, "All words are pegs to hang ideas on." In other words, vocabulary instruction is *not* about students tediously memorizing word lists, but rather developing pegs upon which to hang subject-specific concepts (*mitosis, meiosis, oligarchy, plutocracy, exposition, denouement*) and academic processes (*compare, contrast, synthesize, explain*) so they can focus on thinking about, analyzing, and discussing key concepts, big ideas, and enduring understandings. In the Appendix, you'll find summaries of 14 experimental studies with demonstrated significant effect sizes (improvement index = 11–46) for direct instruction in subject-specific and academic vocabulary across all subject areas, multiple grade levels, and different student populations.

Guiding principles for direct instruction of vocabulary

From these studies, we can distill the following guiding principles for effective vocabulary instruction.

Students acquire new words best when they encounter and use them in a variety of ways.

Several studies have demonstrated that vocabulary acquisition occurs only after students encounter new words in multiple ways, including the following:

- Hearing student-friendly definitions (Vaughn et al., 2017)
- Seeing examples (and nonexamples) of words in sentences (Wood et al., 2018)
- Seeing visual and concrete examples of new words (August et al., 2009; Coyne et al., 2019; Vaughn et al., 2017; Wasik & Bond, 2001)
- Practicing words in conversations with peers (Vaughn et al., 2017)
- Incorporating new words into writing exercises (Lesaux et al., 2014)
- Practicing them in word games (Townsend & Collins, 2009)

McKeown and colleagues (2018), for example, found positive effects for teaching cross-curricular vocabulary terms to mostly low-income middle school students by showing them the words in multiple contexts (e.g., "expose" in relation to radiation, art, and culture), teaching denotations and connotations of each word, and having students incorporate the words into their writing. Students also learned the Latin roots of words (e.g., *fin* in "finite") and morphemes that altered word meanings (e.g., un- and -ed). After teaching 99 words to students over 11 weeks, 6th grade students in the treatment group demonstrated greater gains in word knowledge (improvement index = 26) and reading comprehension (improvement index = 35) than those in a control group taught the same words without multiple opportunities to learn and apply them.

Quality is more important than quantity.

Effective interventions do not seek to barrage students with new words but rather adopt a less-is-more approach, focusing on a limited set of words— anywhere from 3 to 5 target words per week (Lesaux et al., 2014) to 12 to 14 words per week (Carlo et al., 2004). This approach to quality over quantity includes such practices as the following:

- Defining and explaining new words to multilingual, low-income young students as they encounter them during storybook read-aloud sessions (Justice et al., 2005)
- Providing students with prior low levels of achievement opportunities to review target words and use them in peer conversations (Coyne et al., 2019; Pullen et al., 2010)
- Encouraging students (including emergent bilingual students) to use new words in extended writing assignments (Lesaux et al., 2014; Vadasy et al., 2015)

Students benefit from direct instruction in both subject-specific and academic vocabulary terms.

Studies have shown that students benefit from direct instruction of subject-specific terms in science (August et al., 2009; Brown et al., 2010; Tong et al., 2014; Townsend & Collins, 2009), social studies (Townsend & Collins, 2009; Vaughn et al., 2017), and mathematics (Fuchs et al., 2021). Students also benefit from direct instruction in general-purpose academic vocabulary words, including those linked to the following areas:

- Early reading comprehension (e.g., "heaved," "pouted," "surface," "decided," "stale"; Coyne et al., 2019; Justice et al., 2005; Pullen et al., 2010; Wasik & Bond, 2001)
- Reading comprehension for multilingual students (e.g., "famine," "flee," "motive," "optimism," "prospect"; Carlo et al., 2004; Wasik & Bond, 2001)
- Words in everyday reading (e.g., "expose," "refine"; Lesaux et al., 2014; McKeown et al., 2018; Vadasy et al., 2015)

Direct instruction of academic vocabulary helps to close gaps.

Teaching vocabulary benefits all students and appears to close achievement gaps by delivering even greater benefits for low-income students (Kim et al., 2017; Stevens, 2003), multilingual learners (Carlo et al., 2004; Lesaux et al.,

2014; Tong et al., 2014; Vaughn et al., 2017; Wasik & Bond, 2001), and students with reading difficulties (Justice et al., 2005; Townsend & Collins, 2009).

For example, Justice and colleagues (2005) compared the effects of merely exposing kindergarten students to target words during read-aloud sessions versus pausing to explain words to them. Students with rich vocabularies appeared to pick up new words easily via incidental exposure (improvement index = 30). Although those with poor vocabularies learned very few target words through incidental exposure (improvement index = 4), these students made significant gains (improvement index = 41) when teachers paused to explain target words to them. These findings, along with those from a similar study (Coyne et al., 2019), demonstrate that "light-touch" strategies that merely expose students to new words may perpetuate or exacerbate achievement gaps whereas "high-touch" direct instruction of new words can close them.

Students benefit from direct instruction in word analysis and vocabulary learning strategies.

Students must learn thousands of words over the course of their academic careers—far more than can be taught directly. So, teachers must also show students how to *teach themselves* new words by, for example, using context clues to discern connotations and meanings of words or using knowledge of prefixes and suffixes to figure out unfamiliar words. Multiple studies, in fact, have demonstrated positive effects for teaching students to teach themselves new words (Carlo et al., 2004; McKeown et al., 2018; Wood et al., 2018).

Carlo and colleagues (2004), for example, found significant positive effects (improvement index = 13) when Spanish- and English-speaking 5th graders were provided with direct instruction in word analysis and vocabulary learning strategies. Over a 15-week period, students in the treatment group received 30 to 45 minutes of instruction 4 days per week in 12 to 14 target words, along with strategies for using context clues, morphology (i.e., recognizing different forms of words such as "election," "elect," "electing"), and cognates (i.e., words similar in Spanish and English such as "frigid" and *frio*) to infer word meanings. Students in the control group, meanwhile, received business-as-usual instruction without emphasis on vocabulary instruction. Afterward, both multilingual learners and English-only students in the treatment group outperformed those in the control group on measures of word mastery (improvement index = 34) and reading comprehension (improvement index = 19).

Vocabulary instruction should supplement, not supplant, conceptual understanding.

Vocabulary instruction is not rote memorization of words but, rather, ensuring students understand concepts and acquire words as the pegs upon which to hang them. Developing conceptual understanding *prior to* vocabulary instruction can be more effective than teaching concepts through words. For example, Brown and colleagues (2010) compared the effects of providing 5th graders in low-income, highly diverse schools with two different approaches to a science unit on photosynthesis. Students in the treatment group engaged in inquiry-based science units that used everyday language to build their conceptual understanding of photosynthesis prior to learning related terms. Meanwhile, students in the control group learned science concepts and vocabulary concurrently. On an end-of-unit test, those in the treatment group demonstrated significantly better understanding of science concepts (improvement index = 13) than those in the control group. So, if words are the pegs on which to hang ideas, it may be more effective to provide students with ideas first and pegs second.

It is worth noting that vocabulary instruction should not crowd out or replace other forms of teaching—as revealed in an experiment designed to increase 4th and 5th graders' reading comprehension skills through vocabulary instruction (Vadasy et al., 2015). After 14 weeks of vocabulary instruction, students in the treatment group demonstrated significant gains in word knowledge (improvement index = 49) yet minimal gains in reading comprehension (improvement index = 6). Classroom observations revealed that, as teachers in the treatment group ramped up vocabulary instruction, they ramped *down* teaching comprehension. These findings suggest that vocabulary instruction is necessary but not sufficient for deeper learning and should be balanced with teaching conceptual understanding and other skills.

Classroom tips for vocabulary instruction

Taken together, these studies paint a compelling picture of vocabulary instruction as an important strategy, especially when balanced with other strategies that support deeper learning, comprehension, and critical thinking. With this in mind, we offer the following tips for incorporating vocabulary instruction into your classroom.

Unpack standards to identify essential subject-specific vocabulary.

Embedded in most learning standards—especially those that reflect declarative knowledge—are enduring understandings, which, in turn, comprise important concepts that are typically captured in subject-specific vocabulary. If your standards or curriculum guides do not already include vocabulary terms, you'll likely need to extract these from the key concepts embedded in the standards. Doing so helps you to identify the key terms students must know and be able to use fluently to master content standards. Figure 3.1 illustrates the process of moving from a standard to a targeted list of subject-specific vocabulary terms that relate directly to student learning standards.

FIGURE 3.1   A STANDARD UNPACKED TO IDENTIFY KEY VOCABULARY TERMS

STANDARD

- Make observations and/or measurements to provide evidence of the effects of weathering or the rate of erosion by water, ice, wind, or vegetation. (4-ESS2-1, NGSS)

CORE CONCEPTS

- Rainfall helps to shape the land and affects the types of living things found in a region.
- Water, ice, wind, living organisms, and gravity break rocks, soils, and sediments into smaller particles and move them around.

KEY VOCABULARY

- Weathering
- Erosion
- Windspeed
- Deposition
- Sediment

Provide direct instruction in age-appropriate academic vocabulary words.

In addition to subject-specific terms, students encounter many words in academic settings that are less common in everyday speech, such as those that appear frequently in classroom discourse (e.g., "data," "compare," "contrast," "formula") and written text (e.g., "banter," "blissful," "massive," "nonchalant," "saunter"). Vocabulary instruction is, of course, more effective when students encounter words in context. Instead of simply plucking a list of words from the internet, start with unfamiliar words students should run across frequently in class or in texts, and then provide students with explicit opportunities to learn and practice these words.

Teaching essential vocabulary to students is but a first step in developing their understanding of key concepts and ideas. To guide learning from short- to long-term memory, teachers need to provide students with tools and strategies for embedding new words into their own working vocabularies. Here are some strategies that effectively support rich use of academic language and subject-specific vocabulary:

- Help students create a personal dictionary where, following direct instruction, they record and write their own example(s) of how to use new words, which they can refer to later when they need to remember what a word means or how it can be used in context.
- As students learn new words and ways to use them in context, engage them in creating a classroom "word wall," where words are clustered and categorized; this helps students recognize patterns and relationships among words.
- Engage students in "turn and talk" to discuss and explain new words with a partner.

Help students consider new words in multiple ways.

The more ways students can encounter and think about the concepts reflected in new words, the more apt they are to truly learn them. An effective tool to support vocabulary learning is the Frayer model (Frayer et al., 1969; see Figure 3.2), a graphic organizer that prompts students to provide their own definition of a word, list its characteristics, and provide examples and nonexamples. Some modifications of this tool include sketching related images, making personal connections to words, or using them in a sentence. Additional modifications for multilingual learners might include identifying cognates or definitions in their home language.

FIGURE 3.2   THE FRAYER MODEL FOR VOCABULARY INSTRUCTION

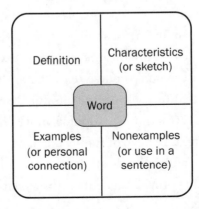

Provide multiple opportunities for students to practice and apply new vocabulary.

New vocabulary is more likely to stick when students have multiple opportunities to practice using words in oral and written communication. Think-pair-share conversations are simple and effective ways for students to use new words and can be particularly helpful for multilingual learners, giving them opportunities to process the meanings of new words in their home language. For example, students might work together to generate a list of examples and nonexamples of new terms (e.g., oligarchy vs. plutocracy). Many studies (e.g., August et al., 2009; Tong et al., 2014; Vadasy et al., 2015) have also shown positive benefits of giving students opportunities to use new words in short writing exercises (e.g., writing about the differences between plutocracies and oligarchies and the conditions that create them).

Teach students how to expand their own vocabulary knowledge with linguistic devices.

Adults and skilled readers tend to discern the meaning of unfamiliar words from context clues, cognates, Latinate derivations, and morphology. You can teach these skills to students by providing them with direct instruction in common prefixes and suffixes (see Figure 3.3). Similarly, you can help students understand common Latinate roots of English words (see Figure 3.4, p. 50).

FIGURE 3.3   COMMON PREFIXES AND SUFFIXES OF ENGLISH WORDS

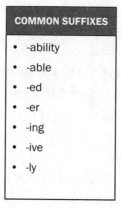

COMMON PREFIXES	COMMON SUFFIXES
• a-	• -ability
• bi-	• -able
• in-	• -ed
• re-	• -er
• un-	• -ing
• under-	• -ive
• super-	• -ly
• trans-	

FIGURE 3.4　COMMON LATIN ROOTS OF ENGLISH WORDS

audi- (hear, sound)	inter- (between)	mal- (bad)	retro- (backward)
bene- (good)	intra- (within)	multi- (many)	san- (healthy)
cent- (hundred)	jur- (law)	neg- (no)	sub- (under)
dict- (say)	liber- (free)	non- (not)	tri- (three)
ex- (out)	lumin- (light)	pan- (all, whole)	uni- (one)
fract- (break)	magn- (great)	quasi- (as if)	vac- (empty)

Strategy 4: Strategy Instruction and Modeling

Strategy instruction and modeling develop procedural knowledge through explicit direct instruction and demonstration of key skills, learning processes, and thinking strategies.

Strategy instruction and modeling means demonstrating for students how to perform specific skills or tasks, such as solving word problems, writing extended essays, reading for comprehension, and reflecting on their learning. Students gain little from muddling through learning new skills on their own but rather benefit from straightforward, step-by-step guidance and modeling of new skills. As with vocabulary instruction, strategy instruction and modeling are a means, not an end, to actual learning. You might think of it as the "I do it" phase within the "I do it, we do it, you do it together, you do it alone" progression of the gradual release of learning model (Fisher & Frey, 2021). One likely reason this technique is so powerful is that learning new skills places significant cognitive demand on students; their brains must toggle back and forth between performing each step in a new process and recalling the steps in sequence.

Fortunately, as students master new processes, their brains begin to translate them into automated scripts or heuristics so they can redirect more mental energy to higher level tasks such as writing creatively, thinking critically, and evaluating solutions to problems. Ultimately, your aim in providing direct instruction and modeling of new skills is to help students develop fluency with key processes so they can engage in the real-life problem-solving, explorations and investigations, and critical-thinking activities we highlight in Chapter 6.

Our review of research identified 23 empirical studies of effective interventions with strategy instruction and modeling at the core of the intervention (see the Appendix). These studies demonstrated moderate to strong effect sizes (improvement index = 8–47) across multiple subject areas, grade levels, and student groups. Students developed mastery of a wide array of procedural knowledge—from basic reading and math skills to more advanced skills, such as reading for comprehension, writing, and solving complex math problems.

Guiding principles for strategy instruction and modeling

The following principles for strategy instruction and modeling emerge from these studies.

Many crucial skills are not intuitive to students and must be taught directly. Our adult brains have automated so many mental processes we can easily forget that, at some point, we had to learn all of those processes, often through direct instruction and hours of painstaking practice. As a result, it can be easy for us to mistakenly assume that many of the skills students need to develop are simple, intuitive, or materialize naturally—whether it's counting on their fingers, solving word problems, extracting key ideas from text, or writing coherent paragraphs. Yet all of these things are actually learned skills, which many students are slow to develop (or may never develop) without direct instruction.

Here's one example. Many students, especially those struggling in mathematics, often try to solve math problems by counting both digits of a formula (e.g., 3 + 5) on their fingers. Tournaki (2003) randomly assigned one group of 2nd grade students to receive direct instruction in a strategy that for most adults seems intuitive. The "minimal addend" strategy starts with the larger of two digits (e.g., 5) and "counts on" from there (e.g., 6, 7, 8). Compared to a control group that engaged in addition drill and practice, teaching this simple skill to students supported learning gains for all students (improvement index = 29), with even greater gains for students with identified learning disabilities (improvement index = 43).

Additional studies offer strong evidence for direct instruction in other simple yet powerful strategies, including the following:

- Showing multilingual students how to extract word meanings from cognates, root words, and base words (improvement index = 13; August et al., 2009)

- Providing 4th and 5th graders with learning disabilities simple routines for planning and writing essays (improvement index = 48; Troia & Graham, 2002)
- Showing students how to apply simple rule-based facts to solve multiplication problems (e.g., 6 x 7 = 6 x 6 + 6; improvement index = 22; Woodward, 2006)

These straightforward interventions had significant effects on student learning, which suggests that without direct instruction, many students will be slow to develop core skills in reading, writing, thinking, and problem-solving—or will never develop them at all.

Strategy instruction is more effective when combined with step-by-step demonstrations.

Effective strategy instruction interventions typically follow a "show and tell" approach, with teachers explaining and demonstrating processes such as the following:

- Showing low-achieving 2nd graders how to use clue words (e.g., "because," "therefore") to identify cause-effect text structure, use graphic organizers to depict these relationships, and employ questioning strategies to review and summarize text (Williams et al., 2007)
- Modeling for racially diverse 3rd grade students how to activate background knowledge, ask questions, search for information, summarize, and organize information graphically while reading nonfiction texts (Guthrie et al., 2004)
- Demonstrating for 5th and 6th graders how to use a "self-monitoring sheet" to set and monitor goals and follow a four-step strategy for writing (i.e., tell what you believe, give three or more reasons, explain each reason, wrap it up; Limpo & Alves, 2014)
- Showing 4th grade students how to improve their writing by creating complex sentences from two or more basic ones—for example, combining "Ralph stuck his head out," "Ralph was in Ryan's pocket," "Ralph looked around," and "Ralph did not know where he was" into "Ralph, who was in Ryan's pocket, did not know where he was, but stuck his head out and looked around" (Saddler & Graham, 2005, p. 46)
- Modeling for middle and high school students how experienced readers use thinking strategies while reading—for example, "When readers tap prior knowledge, they might say to themselves inside their heads, 'I already know that...,' 'This reminds me of...,' or 'This makes me think about...'" (Olson & Land, 2007, p. 279)—as well as providing sentence starters to model

metacognitive thinking (e.g., "My purpose is . . .," "At first I thought ___, but now I think . . .," or "I got lost here because . . ."; Olson & Land, 2007, p. 280)

Students benefit from explicit instruction and demonstration of thinking strategies.

When students are explicitly taught to reflect on prior knowledge before reading, summarize key ideas, and ask themselves questions to support comprehension, it enhances their reading comprehension (Guthrie et al., 2004) and content knowledge (Vaughn et al., 2017). In their study involving nearly 2,000 multilingual learners in a large, urban, low-income district, Olson and colleagues (2017) found positive effects (improvement index = 25) for teaching students to develop a "toolkit" of thinking strategies. The toolkit included reflecting on prior knowledge, asking questions and making predictions, identifying main ideas, self-monitoring comprehension, thinking aloud while reading, and revising one's own thinking. Other studies have reported similar positive effects for teaching thinking skills to improve the writing abilities of 4th and 5th grade students with learning disabilities (Troia & Graham, 2002) and the social studies content knowledge and reading comprehension of multilingual 8th graders (Vaughn et al., 2017). These findings all suggest that thinking skills are neither innate nor intuitive for many students, but rather something that can (and should) be taught.

Classroom tips for strategy instruction and modeling

Together, these studies illustrate that direct instruction can help students develop the foundational skills they need to engage in more complex, high-level learning. With this in mind, we offer the following classroom tips for teaching and modeling skills to your students.

Identify the skills students need to master their learning goals and teach these directly.

Start with your student learning goals and unpack the processes and thinking skills they need to achieve those goals. Some may be simple step-by-step processes, like those used to solve two-column addition problems (e.g., line up problems, add the right-hand column first, carry the 1). In other cases, sub-skills may be nested within larger procedures—for example, learning how to engage in close-reading strategies as a key to reading comprehension. A good place to begin, of course, is with your standards and the associated procedural knowledge and skills students must master to achieve them. Figure 3.5 illustrates the process of extracting key skills from a standard.

FIGURE 3.5   A STANDARD UNPACKED TO IDENTIFY TEACHABLE SKILLS

STANDARD

Students will be able to analyze the main ideas and supporting details presented in diverse media and formats and explain how ideas clarify a topic, text, or issue under study.

PROCEDURAL KNOWLEDGE

- Summarizing and synthesizing text to highlight main ideas
- Identifying supporting details
- Making connections between main ideas and supporting details

SKILLS

- How to summarize and synthesize text
- How to use a graphic organizer to connect supporting details and main ideas
- How to analyze supporting details for validity, coherence, and logic

---

Show and tell when demonstrating new skills and procedures to students.

Studies of talent development (e.g., Bloom, 1985) have shown that following exemplars and models—such as copying the work of a master artist, emulating how a tennis pro hits a serve, or watching a YouTube video of a professional guitarist playing a riff—is often critical to learning new skills. None of this is surprising given what we know about dual-coding theory; we learn best when we see a process and hear it explained. So, once you've identified the critical skills you want students to learn, consider how to *show and tell* the new procedure to students. It's not enough to tell students that they should, for example, follow a four-step process for writing a persuasive paragraph. Show them each step of the process as well (e.g., "Our first step is to state what we believe. With this step, we want to come right out and state our argument. So, I might write something like, 'I believe we should ban plastic drinking straws.'").

Provide direct instruction in thinking strategies.

Successful learners develop thinking skills that generally fall into two overlapping categories: cognitive and metacognitive thinking strategies (see Figure 3.6).

Cognitive thinking is how we focus on new learning, for example, by connecting it with prior knowledge, distilling the gist from a text, analyzing and evaluating ideas, making decisions, and solving problems. *Metacognitive thinking,* on the other hand, is thinking about thinking. It's the voice in our heads that helps us assess where we are with our learning. It says things like, "Wait, I don't get this. I need to get back on track. And I'm not sure if my answer makes sense."

FIGURE 3.6   COGNITIVE AND METACOGNITIVE THINKING STRATEGIES

COGNITIVE STRATEGIES		METACOGNITIVE STRATEGIES	
Analysis	What kind of problem is this? Which strategy should I use to solve it?	Planning	What are my goals? What do I need to do to accomplish this task well?
Comprehension	What does this mean? Does it make sense to me?	Monitoring comprehension	What do I still not understand?
Connection	How does this relate to what I already know?	Monitoring progress	Am I still on track?
Recall	Do I remember what I've learned? What steps do I need to follow?	Evaluating procedures	Did I do that right? Did I forget anything?
Summarization	What's the main idea? Can I express it in my own words?	Evaluating outcomes	Does that answer look right? What do I need to revise?

This ability to think about thinking is a learned skill that often distinguishes successful from struggling learners. You can use think-alouds to model metacognitive strategies, walking your students through situations such as the following:

- How experienced readers approach new texts (e.g., "Can I infer from the title what this article is about? What do I know about the subject already?")
- How experienced writers reflect on their writing (e.g., "Have I made an interesting point? Do my details support my arguments?")
- How successful students tackle complex math problems (e.g., "What kind of problem is this? Have I solved similar problems? What strategies did I use to solve them?")

Strategy 5: Visualizations and Concrete Examples

Visual representations and examples—diagrams, graphic organizers, manipulatives, worked examples, videos, and simulations—support visual and verbal (dual-coding) comprehension of new ideas.

The well-worn phrase "a picture is worth a thousand words" reflects a key concept from cognitive science, namely, the dual-coding theory of information processing, which suggests our brains process information more efficiently and effectively when they receive visual images paired with verbal guidance. It's not surprising that several empirical studies support pairing verbal and visual learning to help students focus on new learning. Our review of research yielded 23 empirical studies with strong effect sizes (improvement index = 11–45; see the Appendix for interventions that helped students visualize new learning with graphics, images, concrete examples, and worked-out problems in language arts, mathematics, and science).

Guiding principles for visualizations and concrete examples

Here are the guiding principles for visualizations and concrete examples that emerge from these studies.

Illustrations, animations, and manipulatives support conceptual understanding.

Several studies have demonstrated positive effects for using visual representations to help students develop conceptual understanding of new ideas and skills, such as the following:

- Helping multilingual students understand science concepts (August et al., 2009)
- Using number lines, circles, and manipulatives to develop elementary students' conceptual understanding of fractions (Bottge et al., 2014; Fuchs, Geary et al., 2013)
- Using computer-based animations to support middle schoolers' understanding of algebraic concepts (Scheiter et al., 2010)

Visualizations are most helpful during early phases of learning (i.e., while students are focusing on new learning). Once students fully grasp science and math concepts, it's often more efficient for them to consider abstract depictions of math problems and verbal representations of the science concepts. For example, once students develop a visual understanding of addition, math manipulatives are no longer necessary—and far less efficient than simply engaging in the abstract depiction of $2 + 3 = 5$.

Students better comprehend abstract concepts illustrated with concrete examples.

Research has also demonstrated the benefits of helping students understand abstract principles by illustrating them with familiar, concrete examples. For example, Bulgren and colleagues (2000) found significant positive effects (improvement index = 34) using a "concept anchoring routine," a visual aid designed to help students link abstract concepts to a familiar, concrete example, such as relating warm-blooded animals' ability to regulate body temperature to temperature control systems in modern buildings. Similarly, students were taught about *commensalism* (relationships between living creatures in which one benefits without benefiting or harming another) through a story about a lemonade stand. In another experiment, Scheiter and colleagues (2010) demonstrated the benefits (improvement index = 37) of using computer animations to help students understand algebraic concepts with the "concreteness fading" method, which begins with teachers sharing concrete examples (typically three) and gradually replacing these with abstract representations (Fyfe et al., 2014).

Studying worked-out examples helps students develop new skills and understandings.

Worked-out examples are another visual representation with demonstrated positive effects on learning, especially when students are learning complex, multistep skills and procedures. For example, Mwangi and Sweller (1998) found that 3rd grade students developed better math problem-solving skills when they followed worked-out examples of two-step problem-solving procedures (improvement index = 44). Notably, though, worked-out problems only enhanced learning when offered side-by-side with problems students were solving, not at the end of the problem. This is likely because end-of-problem examples require students to flip back and forth between the solution and the problem they are solving instead of unpacking the solution method one step at a time, with examples of correct procedures provided in a side-by-side format.

Other researchers have found similar benefits for providing side-by-side worked-out examples to 5th graders solving multistep math problems (Star &

Rittle-Johnson, 2009) and 7th graders learning multistep algebraic problem solving (Rittle-Johnson & Star, 2007). It is worth noting that the benefits of worked-out examples appear to increase with task complexity; worked-out examples offer few benefits for simple tasks but significant benefits for complex tasks (Kalyuga et al., 2001). That is likely because referring to examples eases students' initial cognitive load for learning. However, as they become more proficient with procedural knowledge, the positive effects of worked-out examples diminish in favor of learning with self-guided exploration and practice.

Schematics help guide and support procedural knowledge.

As we've noted, learning any new skill requires significant mental bandwidth to toggle back and forth between mastering each step of the process while simultaneously attempting to remember the process itself. It's not surprising that visual aids, such as diagrams of the various steps required for complex procedures, have been found to significantly enhance student learning outcomes. For example, Swanson and colleagues' (2013) study involved elementary students with math difficulties (i.e., those testing below the 25th percentile on standardized assessments). Students who were given a visual schematic (i.e., a diagram that supported each step of a five-step process for solving word problems) outperformed those who were only taught the process without the aid of the diagram (improvement index = 22).

As it turns out, engaging students in creating their *own* visual representations of problems can also be a powerful aid to learning. A study involving 5th grade students (Terwel et al., 2009) found that students who co-created their own visual representations (in this case, illustrations of the mathematical concept of percentages) outperformed those who followed a teacher-provided visual representation (improvement index = 24).

Classroom tips for visualizations and concrete examples

Scientific research offers no evidence for "learning styles" or any benefits for classifying students as visual, verbal, kinesthetic, or other learning style and attempting to match their learning experiences accordingly (Pashler et al., 2008). If anything, scientific studies—including those highlighted here—show that *all* students benefit from pairing visual with verbal learning, precisely because their brains are hardwired to absorb information more readily when they receive it visually and verbally. With this in mind, we offer the following practical tips for using visualizations and concrete examples in your classroom.

Consider what you want students to see and visualize while they learn.

As you develop unit and lesson plans, consider exactly what you want students to see and be able to visualize in their minds as they learn. Maybe it's the top-heavy hierarchy of the Mayan civilization, the frequencies of ultraviolet and infrared light waves, the difference between linear and nonlinear curves, or Shakespeare's Globe Theater. We suggest using a T-chart (see Figure 3.7) to define what you want students to learn (the left-hand column) and what you want them to visualize (the right-hand column). Creating such a list will help you identify the graphics, images, videos, and manipulatives you can provide students to help them process new learning, visually and verbally. You can expand on this list by identifying two particular types of visualizations: concrete examples and schematics.

FIGURE 3.7   T-CHART PLANNING FOR VISUALIZATIONS

WHAT DO I NEED STUDENTS TO LEARN?	WHAT DO I WANT STUDENTS TO VISUALIZE?
How to perform two-column addition	Worked-out examples of two-column addition
How evaporation, condensation, and precipitation create a water cycle	A diagram of the water cycle, including water evaporating, condensing in clouds, and precipitating back to Earth
How to revise sentences to make them stronger and more succinct	"Before and after" sentences with passive verbs versus strong ones

Illustrate abstract ideas with familiar, concrete examples.

In addition to visual imagery, consider how you can help students translate abstract ideas into concrete examples and manipulatives. Perhaps use an analogy of trading cards to describe supply and demand? Or a manipulative (e.g., a globe) to illustrate how Earth circling the Sun on a tilted axis creates seasons? A good rule of thumb is to provide three concrete examples for each abstract idea—for example, illustrating the concept of predation with examples of owls eating mice, coyotes eating rabbits, and birds eating insects. Although identifying visualizations and concrete examples takes time, time devoted to planning how to show and tell students what they should learn is time well spent. As the research demonstrates, such planning and preparation greatly increase students' ability to comprehend and retain key concepts.

Help students visualize processes with schematics and diagrams.
As students learn multistep processes (e.g., how to write a paragraph, solve a word problem, complete a research project), provide them with diagrams or tools that help them recall and follow the steps of the process. You also can provide schematics or diagrams to support students' comprehension of complex phenomena, processes, or frameworks they are studying in science, social studies, and language arts, such as the water cycle, the law of supply and demand, or the elements of story plot. Most units of study, in fact, aim to help students comprehend complex phenomena or master multistep processes, which students will more readily master when provided some form of visualization. Schematics can be even more powerful when students create their own—for example, creating a diagram to guide them through a process or to capture and reflect their own understanding of complex phenomena.

Final Thoughts: Helping Students Focus Their Working Memories

At the beginning of this chapter, we noted that working memories have some limitations—including how much information students can process at once and the brain's natural tendency to "close without saving." That's the bad news. The good news is that our brains have an amazing ability to do two things at once—namely, process visual and verbal information simultaneously—as well as to turn complex processes into automated scripts that we can execute fluently and effortlessly. The strategies highlighted in this chapter can help your students overcome the limitations of their working memories by engaging them in learning experiences that tap into these amazing features of their brains and, in so doing, make learning more efficient, less effortful, and more enjoyable.

These strategies are not ends in themselves but rather ways to help students develop the foundational knowledge and skills required for deeper, more enriching learning experiences. At this point, in fact, we are just halfway through the long and winding journey learning must take before finding a home in students' long-term memories. In the next chapter, we'll explore and explain proven strategies for the next, vitally important phase of the learning process: helping students consolidate and process new information, which is to say, *make sense of it.*

4

Helping Students
Make Sense of Learning

Take a moment to consider what you've learned from this book so far. There may be many ideas and concepts from previous chapters swirling around your mind, including academic vocabulary, Latin roots, schematic diagrams, and cognitive strategies. It's probably still a bit of a jumble—a collection of disorganized thoughts that have yet to sink in. At this point, your brain has converted one form of electrical impulses (sensory input) into a new set of electrical patterns (memories) through a process called *encoding*. Yet these new thoughts and ideas, called *memory traces,* remain scattered in your brain. Most likely, you're not yet sure what to do with them or how to apply them in your classroom.

What's happening in your brain right now is you have begun to store new information as memory traces but have to yet to arrange them in your mind, a process called *consolidation* (Brown et al., 2014). To put it in plain language, you have yet to *make sense of learning*. Without consolidation, what you've learned from this book so far can easily be forgotten.

Your students face the same challenge when focusing on new learning in your classroom: they've learned new skills, concepts, words, and ways of thinking but have yet to fully process them, become fluent with them, or embed them as new habits of mind.

In this chapter, we'll explore how the brain consolidates and makes sense of new learning and the classroom interventions proven to help students make sense of new learning—to ensure this new learning continues the journey from short-term working memory to long-term memory.

What the Research Says

What does cognitive science have to tell us about making sense of new learning? Let's look at what studies have revealed.

The brain encodes information in "messy" neural networks

Although the process of encoding is not fully understood, it appears to be rather messy. For starters, the brain doesn't store information into tidy, carefully labeled mental folders (e.g., words beginning with the letter *A*, memories of Grandma, summer activities circa 1981). Rather, new memories and knowledge are stored in complex neural networks—interwoven webs of ideas, memories, and skills. These neural connections can become more evident as we attempt to retrieve knowledge. For example, it's often easier to generate word *associations* (e.g., mascots of teams in a sports division) than *lists* (e.g., teams with mascots that begin with the letter *a*). This is why a smell (apple pie) can evoke a particular place (Grandma's house) and why returning to one's childhood neighborhood can trigger a flood of memories (using sticks to sling green apples).

The more elaborately new learning is encoded, the more likely it is to be retained

In one lab experiment (Medina, 2008), researchers gave two randomly selected groups of participants lists of words. Neither group was directed to memorize their list; the first group was asked to identify the number of words on the list that contained letters with diagonal strokes, and the second was asked to rate how much they liked or disliked each of the words listed. The second group, called on to think about what each word signified and what feelings they had about it, later recalled two to three times as many words as the first, which suggests that the more elaborately we encode information—including personalizing it—the more likely we are to recall it.

Students are more likely to consolidate information they think about

Cognitive science confirms that individuals are more apt to remember what they think about. As a classic experiment (Hyde & Jenkins, 1969) documented, subjects who were given a list of words and asked to consider whether they had pleasant or unpleasant associations with those words (e.g., "garbage") were more likely to remember those words than subjects who were asked to count the number of letters or the instances of the letter *e* in them in the same list of words. As cognitive scientist Daniel Willingham explains, "There is one factor that trumps most others in determining what is remembered: what you think about when you encounter the material" (2003, p. 78). The implication here is fairly straightforward: to learn something, students must think about it as they're learning it.

Students consolidate learning by connecting it with prior knowledge

A key process at the heart of consolidation is connecting new knowledge with prior knowledge. For example, you are likely most able to recall the parts of this book you could relate to your own prior knowledge and experience. Making these mental connections helped you begin to consolidate your learning, anchoring it to existing knowledge and memories. The same is true for students: the more they can connect new knowledge with prior knowledge, such as relating history to current events or making personal connections to literature, the more likely they will be to consolidate their learning.

Students consolidate learning by clustering and categorizing it

Working memories can hold only a limited amount of information at once. Through the process of consolidation, your brain overcomes this limitation by grouping disparate bits of knowledge and skills into larger groups, categories, and coherent scripts (Bailey & Pransky, 2014). For example, instead of attempting to understand the individual properties of helium, neon, argon, krypton, xenon, and radon, you might categorize them as inert gases. Similarly, students consolidate learning a new skill by bundling smaller steps together into larger processes, scripts, and heuristics (Brown et al., 2014). For example, practice fielding ground balls in baseball or softball consolidates a multistep process—hop over to the ground ball, keep glove down, catch ball, remove ball from glove, pivot on back foot, point shoulder, and throw to first base—into a single fluid process: scoop and throw to first base.

Properly timed feedback supports initial acquisition of new knowledge and skills

During initial attempts to master new knowledge and skills, formative feedback supports consolidation by helping students see what they have yet to master or automate effectively. Such feedback, however, is generally more helpful when slightly delayed—for example, when players receive pointers only after taking a handful of jump shots on the basketball court or students get answers after taking a quiz rather than after each quiz question (Butler & Roediger, 2008). As a review of more than 131 studies found, somewhat counterintuitively, in fully one-third of these studies, feedback was associated with detrimental effects on learning; this is likely because when feedback is too immediate or too frequent, it can interrupt the creation of automated scripts or become a crutch, preventing reflection on learning—both of which result in superficial encoding and weaker consolidation of learning (Kluger & DeNisi, 1996).

The brain needs occasional timeouts to pause and process

Research also suggests that working memories tend to time out after 5 to 10 minutes (for young people) and 10 to 20 minutes for adults (Souza, 2011). One reason for this, as noted in Chapter 3, is that our brains are essentially lazy, always eager to revert back to "low-effort mode" (Kahneman, 2011). Hence, after a few minutes of concentration, our brains need a change of pace—an opportunity to cluster new learning into larger concepts, focus on something else, or experience a change of emotional valence (e.g., switching from serious thinking to an amusing anecdote). If teachers fail to give students these little breaks, their brains are apt to take them anyway. You might be teaching, but they won't be learning. Hence, attempting to cram as much teaching as possible into a single class period is counterproductive; students retain more when given time to process and apply new learning.

In this chapter, we'll explore three evidence-based teaching strategies that can help you translate these guiding principles of memory consolidation into effective student learning experiences.

Strategy 6: High-Level Questions and Student Explanations

High-level questions and student explanations support consolidation of learning through cognitive and metacognitive processing of new knowledge and skills.

The operative term here is *high-level* questions. Low-level recall questions may be helpful to check for understanding or serve as retrieval practice (as we'll discuss in Chapter 5) yet do little to help students make sense of their learning.

The questioning strategies we'll highlight here go beyond quizzing students; instead, they help students to make sense of their learning by thinking about it, connecting it to prior learning, and clustering learning into larger concepts.

Student explanations play a similar cognitive role. When students share their thinking and explain their problem-solving strategies, they must actively think about what they're learning—in effect, slowing down, thinking about what they are doing, and, as a result, encoding learning more elaborately and effectively. Our research review (see the Appendix) identified 17 empirical studies that have demonstrated significant positive effect sizes (improvement index = 14–47) for interventions that support student learning with high-level questions and student explanations across all grade levels, subject areas, and student groups.

Guiding principles for high-level questions and student explanations

Here are some guiding principles for high-level questions and student explanations that emerge from these studies.

Questions that prompt students to think about their learning support better learning outcomes.

High-level questions that prompt students to think about, reflect on, and consolidate their learning are powerful (Clariana & Koul, 2006; King, 1991; Kramarski & Mevarech, 2003; Williams et al., 2007; Zhou & Yadav, 2017). For example, Kramarski and Mevarech (2003) compared the effects of four different conditions for 8th graders learning linear graphs:

1. Cooperative learning with high-level questions
2. Individual learning with high-level questions
3. Cooperative learning without questions
4. Individual learning without questions

The high-level questions included prompts for comprehension (e.g., "What is the trend of the graph?"), strategic thinking (e.g., "What strategy, tactic, or principle can be used to solve the problem or complete the task?"), and connecting with prior knowledge (e.g., "How is this problem similar or different than one you've solved before?"). After 10 days of instruction, post-tests revealed that students who had been provided high-level questions—whether working in groups or individually—significantly outperformed (improvement index = 28) those who worked in teams or individually to solve problems without the benefit of high-level questions to discuss or consider.

Encouraging students to explain their own thinking supports consolidation of new learning.

Several studies have reported positive effects for encouraging students to provide self-explanations while processing and consolidating learning—for example, thinking aloud while solving math problems (Fuchs et al., 2016; Tajika et al., 2007), explaining their reasoning for solutions to math problems (Fuchs et al., 2014), thinking aloud while reading (Olson et al., 2012, 2017), and generating explanations for new learning of science facts (Scruggs et al., 1994). Fuchs and colleagues (2016), for example, found that low-achieving 4th graders who were encouraged to provide high-quality explanations for their solutions to fraction word problems demonstrated significantly greater math problem-solving skills (improvement index = 42) than students who solved the same problems without self-explanations. Similarly, a series of studies conducted with racially diverse, low-income, multilingual students (e.g., Olson et al., 2012, 2017) found significant positive effects for a "cognitive strategies" approach to reading and writing instruction (improvement index = 14–25). Students were provided think-aloud prompts to discuss with a partner (e.g., "At first I thought ___, but now I think ___" and "So, the big idea is ___"), which helped them consolidate the meaning of complex texts (Olson et al., 2012, p. 336).

Showing students how to ask reflective questions supports consolidation of learning.

There is some research support for showing students how to ask high-level questions while developing problem-solving skills (King, 1991) and reading for comprehension (Guthrie et al., 2004; Olson et al., 2012, 2017). King (1991) compared the effects of three different conditions for 5th grade students working in pairs to solve computer-assisted problems. The first group was given strategic questions (e.g., "What is our plan?" "What do we know about the problem so far?" "Do we need a different strategy?") to ask each other while working in pairs to solve logic and spatial reasoning problems (e.g., identifying the proper sequence for a machine to create a product). The second group was instructed to ask each other questions during problem solving but was not given specific questions to ask. The control group worked in pairs to solve the problems but was not instructed to ask questions. The strategic questioners significantly outperformed the unguided questioners (improvement index = 40) as well as students in the control group (improvement index = 34), demonstrating the benefits of providing students with strategic questions to support their consolidation of learning.

Cold-calling techniques are more effective than voluntary response techniques.

Voluntary response techniques (i.e., calling on students who raise their hands) create something of an 80/20 rule in most classrooms: roughly 80 percent of class discussions are dominated by just 20 percent of students (Jones, 1990). Typically, students who do most of the talking in classrooms are already high performers; low-performing students recede into the background and engage in classroom discussions at progressively lower rates (Good et al., 1987). Rather than calling only on students who raise their hands, teachers should "cold call"—posing high-level questions and randomly calling on individual students. As it turns out, simply believing there's a chance they may be called on in class improves student effort and retention of learning. For example, a study of college students (McDougall & Granby, 1996) found that students who were told they would be called upon at random to answer questions during class read more pages before class, spent more time preparing for class, and recalled more information from readings (improvement index = 36) than a control group who expected the instructor to use voluntary responses only.

Quality of questions is more important than quantity.

Finally, it's worth noting that effective interventions that incorporate high-level questions and student explanations tend to reflect a less-is-more approach; typically, teachers pose just a handful of high-level questions rather than barrage students with multiple questions. In fact, the *quantity* of questions teachers pose appears to be inversely related to their *quality*. An observational study in college classrooms (Larson & Lovelace, 2013) found that professors who posed a high number of questions asked predominantly low-level questions. In short, you can help students consolidate their learning by asking a select number of thoughtful, high-level questions and providing ample time for students to consider these questions and respond to them.

Classroom tips for high-level questions and student explanations

Posing high-level questions to students and encouraging them to make their thinking visible through self-explanations helps them process and consolidate their learning by ensuring they think about and reflect on it. With this in mind, we offer the following tips for embedding high-level questions and student explanations in student learning experiences.

Plan high-level questions to scaffold student thinking about their learning.

As you build unit and lesson plans, consider what you want students to think about while they're learning. What new concepts must they grasp? What ideas should they connect? What cause-and-effect relationships should they consider? What nuances must they reflect on to master new skills and procedures? Next, identify a short list of questions you can pose or provide them to help them think about the ideas, concepts, relationships, and nuances of what they are learning. Embed these in your lesson plans.

Prompt students to offer explanations and make their thinking visible.

Your questions should also prompt students to offer explanations, develop thinking skills, and make their thinking visible—a technique sometimes referred to as "elaborative interrogation" (Scruggs et al., 1994). In simple terms, elaborative interrogation prompts students to consider *why* something works or is plausible—"How exactly does that work?" "Why should that be true?" "What if it weren't true?" (McDaniel & Donnelly, 1996). For example, you might ask students to consider *why* it works to cross-multiply fractions, *how exactly* releasing compressed air cools a room, or *what if* Hannibal had made it across the Alps with his elephants and army. One easy way to build elaborative interrogation into learning is with the Golden Question: "What makes you say that?" (Pearsall & Harris, 2019). This simple question makes thinking visible, helps students reflect on their learning, and works for any grade level or subject area.

Use cold calling (and re-calling) to ensure all students think about their learning.

Calling only on students who raise their hands in response to questions you pose typically results in just a small handful of your students doing most of the talking while the rest passively observe—likely doing little to think about or consolidate their learning. For many teachers and students, a shift to cold calling can be a radical departure from previous practice, so you may need to prepare your students for the change. Explain why you want to involve everyone in the discussion and reassure them that the purpose of classroom dialogue is not to make them regurgitate correct answers or evaluate them, but to help everyone make sense of their learning by sharing their ideas and current understandings. To make clear you are calling on students randomly and not seeking to embarrass anyone (or playing favorites), you can draw names on sticks, call numbers, or use a random selection app to ensure you are truly cold calling on everyone. Initially, some students may not feel prepared to respond, but you still want them to think about their learning. So, if you allow anyone to take a pass, let them know you'll return to them later because you want to hear their thoughts. When you return to them, invite them to build on and reflect on what they've heard from their peers.

Use wait time to give your students (and yourself) opportunities to think about questions.

When asking questions, be sure to provide plenty of wait time before calling on students—both after you pose a question and after students respond to your questions. The optimal wait time is at least three seconds for both periods (Rowe, 1986). At first, even a brief pause may feel like an eternity, especially if you're accustomed to rapid-fire questioning. Yet each pause is essential to provide students with time to think about the question you've posed and help them begin to consolidate their learning into an answer. To ensure you provide three seconds of wait time, you may need to count to three in your own head before calling on students, perhaps using an internal rhyme or jingle to ensure you wait long enough (e.g., "I'm going to count to three while students think deeply"). Wait time serves another important purpose for teachers: it can reveal when a question fails to prompt students to think about their learning. If students can immediately respond to your questions without putting much thought into them (e.g., "When was the War of 1812?"), then your questions are probably too simplistic. Providing wait time after a student response is a way to invite other students to connect *their* ideas to what they've heard from a peer. Using a prompt like "Let's all think for a moment how we might connect to or extend that idea . . ." prior to pausing for a few seconds and then calling on another student can result in deeper thinking, make more connections, and show students that they (and not just you) can play an active role in making sense of learning.

Give students opportunities to respond to questions and explain their thinking with their peers.

Many of the studies in our sample posed questions to students in pairs or small (three- to four-person) groups. Doing so provides a safe space for students to collect their thoughts, make their thinking visible, hear how peers are making sense of their own learning, and check their understandings with each other. For emergent multilingual learners, small groups or pairs can also provide opportunities to process ideas in their home language. Later, we will examine peer-assisted consolidation of learning more closely, showing you how to use small groups to ensure all students (not just a vocal few) have opportunities to respond to high-level questions and explain their thinking.

Strategy 7: Guided Initial Application with Formative Feedback

Guided initial application with formative feedback helps students consolidate new skills and procedural knowledge effectively and accurately.

After helping students develop new skills and procedural knowledge through strategy instruction and modeling, you need to give them ample support, guidance, and feedback during their initial attempts to translate what they are beginning to learn into action—that is, as they consolidate their learning and begin to develop automaticity with new skills. This strategy aligns closely to the "we do it" stage within the "I do it," "we do it," "you do it together," "you do it alone" gradual release of responsibility model (Fisher & Frey, 2021), and the "guided practice" stage found in both explicit direct instruction (Hollingsworth & Ybarra, 2017) and mastery teaching (Hunter, 1982). Basically, as students initially learn to apply a new skill, it is important to observe them and provide feedback to help them develop this new skill accurately and effectively. Our review of research yielded 11 empirical studies (see the Appendix) that have demonstrated significant positive effect sizes (improvement index = 11–49) for guided initial application with formative feedback across all grade levels, multiple subject areas, and student groups. Guided initial application with formative feedback is often a close companion to strategy instruction and modeling, as it has been primarily shown to support mastery of procedural knowledge (i.e., learning new skills and processes).

Guiding principles for guided initial application with formative feedback

These studies yield the following principles for guided initial application with formative feedback.

Guided application should be "front-loaded" with direct strategy instruction and modeling.

Several studies have reported positive effects for interventions that integrated strategy instruction and modeling with guided initial application and formative feedback (e.g., Cardelle-Elawar, 1990; Coyne et al., 2019; Fuchs et al., 2009,

2010; Vadasy & Sanders, 2010; Vaughn et al., 2006). At the risk of stating the obvious, students are more successful in their initial attempts to apply new skills when they receive explicit instruction in and modeling of the skills, procedures, and strategies in question. Strategy instruction and guided application are often interspersed with teachers continuously reteaching and remodeling skills, especially for students who initially struggled with a new skill. For example, an intervention in which teachers engaged in "echo reading"—rereading challenging lines of text to students and asking them to repeat those lines aloud—was found to significantly improve the outcomes (improvement index = 30) of previously low-performing kindergarten students (Vadasy & Sanders, 2010).

Students benefit from observation and tailored feedback when first applying new skills.

This phase of learning—as students attempt to master new procedural knowledge—is a precarious moment in the learning process. If students develop misunderstandings or learn skills incorrectly, they are apt to grow frustrated and fall farther behind. So, as they begin to master and automate new skills, it's vital to observe them and provide real-time feedback tailored to their learning needs. Not surprisingly, numerous studies point to the benefits of tailored feedback early in the learning process to ensure students start off on the right track. For example, in a large-scale study with nearly 3,000 students, Roschelle and colleagues (2016) assessed the benefits of an online homework tool that provided personalized hints and timely feedback during 7th graders' initial attempts to master multistep math problems. Students who used the online tool outperformed those who engaged in traditional in-class instruction and homework assignments without feedback or personalized guidance (improvement index = 7). Notably, below-average students benefited even more from the tailored feedback (improvement index = 11), which suggests that individualized, real-time feedback is a powerful strategy for reducing achievement gaps. These findings and those of several other studies conducted in racially diverse settings (Coyne et al., 2019; Fuchs et al., 2009, 2010; Fuchs, Geary, et al., 2013; Roschelle et al., 2016; Vadasy & Sanders, 2008, 2010; Vaughn et al., 2006) demonstrate the power of close observation and tailored feedback during initial application of new learning.

Formative feedback should support student reflection and thinking.

Feedback tends to be more powerful when teachers do not simply spoon-feed correct answers to students but rather encourage them to reflect on their learning and consider how to correct their errors. For example, in one intervention, teachers provided individually tailored feedback that supported consolidation of learning math problem-solving skills through reflection (e.g., "What is the key error?" "Why do you think you made this error?" "Which type of information do you need to solve the problem?"). Low-income, emergent bilingual 6th grade students provided with this type of feedback significantly outperformed those who received correct-answer feedback only (improvement index = 49; Cardelle-Elawar, 1990, p. 168). Similarly, Fuchs and colleagues (2010) explored the benefits of *deliberate practice*—students working with tutors to review their error patterns and apply a new strategy to correct their answers. Racially diverse, low-income 3rd grade students with math difficulties who engaged in deliberate practice significantly outperformed students whose tutors gave only correct-answer feedback (improvement index = 23).

Clariana and Koul (2006) compared the effects of providing high school science students with three different forms of feedback:

- *Delayed feedback,* such as providing access to correct answers at the end of a workbook
- *Correct-response immediate feedback,* such as providing "scratch-off" access to correct answers to multiple-choice questions
- *Multiple-try immediate feedback,* such as accompanying incorrect "scratch-off" answers with "try again" messages

When students were tested later with verbatim and paraphrased test items, students in both the delayed and immediate correct-answer feedback groups outperformed those who received multiple-try feedback and those who received no feedback on verbatim test items (improvement index = 32 and 24, respectively). However, on paraphrased test items, students receiving multiple-try feedback outperformed all other groups (e.g., improvement index = 24 versus text-only). Clariana and Koul concluded that students likely benefited from multiple-try feedback because memory consolidation requires making multiple mental connections to new learning. Thus, feedback that encourages students to think about learning supports greater conceptual understanding.

Once students develop conceptual understanding, progress feedback aids automation.

As students begin to develop fluency with new skills, you can move from prompting them to pause and reflect on their learning toward offering more progress feedback (i.e., telling students if an answer is correct or incorrect). Fuchs, Geary, and colleagues (2013) compared the effects of two different forms of feedback on the mathematics learning of racially diverse, low-income, low-achieving 1st graders. The first group received daily tutoring in number knowledge followed by five minutes of nonspeeded practice with feedback designed to help them reflect on key principles of number knowledge learned during whole-class instruction. The second group received the same tutoring but engaged in five minutes of daily speeded practice during which they attempted to answer as many questions correctly as possible while receiving corrective (i.e., right or wrong answer) feedback. The control group received no special tutoring or additional practice sessions. Not surprisingly, both tutoring groups outperformed the control group; however, the students who engaged in speeded practice with corrective feedback made greater gains (improvement index = 24) than those who engaged in nonspeeded practice with formative feedback (improvement index = 8). These findings suggest that once students have consolidated learning, we actually want them to *stop thinking* about each step of the process and develop automaticity. For example, once they can decode sound-symbol connections we want them to read words fluently. Once they grasp math concepts, we want them to automatically recall math facts. With this in mind, to help students develop automaticity, try shifting from prompting them to think about their learning to instead giving them time to practice with progress feedback.

Giving three correct responses during initial application supports mastery.

Three really is the magic number. Students achieve the greatest success when they can successfully demonstrate a new skill at least three times during an initial application session (Rawson & Dunlosky, 2011). This learning principle was, in fact, built into a software program that demonstrated positive outcomes for thousands of students (Roschelle et al., 2016) by providing them with repeated practice and feedback on new problems until they solved the same problem correctly three times. Compared to a control group of students that engaged in traditional homework assignments without ensuring proficiency in new skills three times over, students using the software demonstrated small but statistically significant gains in learning on end-of-year standardized math tests (improvement index = 7).

Classroom tips for guided initial application with formative feedback

Research demonstrates the power of observing students during their initial attempts to consolidate new skills and providing them with formative feedback. Formative feedback supports conceptual understanding, corrects misconceptions and error patterns, and helps students develop proficiency and automaticity with new skills and procedural knowledge. Here are some tips to help you translate these principles into effective learning experiences for your students.

Observe students during initial application of new learning.

You wouldn't want your tennis coach to show you how to put topspin on your serve, then hand you a basket of balls and say before walking away, "Now you try it; I'll check in later to see where your balls landed." Any self-respecting coach would, of course, watch you closely during your initial attempts to apply a skill so they could offer pointers. Yet walking away from students during their initial attempts to master new skills is, in effect, what teachers do if they give an assignment that introduces a new skill or procedure and fail to observe students as they first begin to apply the skill. So, during students' first attempts to apply new skills (the "we do it" phase of learning), it's important to observe their work in progress. You can do this, of course, by walking the room and looking over students' shoulders during initial application, whether it's solving equations, conjugating irregular verbs, or writing a strong topic sentence. You can also use "flipped lessons," recording explanatory videos students can watch at home and then devoting class time to observing students and providing them with feedback as they apply new skills.

Identify error patterns and provide targeted feedback to students.

The real power of observation, of course, is that it allows teachers to target feedback to students' learning needs. The following questions are drawn from Cardelle-Elawar's (1990) effective intervention for teaching mathematics to middle school students. This is a useful template for reflection to help you target feedback to student needs while ensuring the feedback itself remains formative, helping students in turn to reflect on and think about their own learning:

1. "What is the key error?"
2. "What is the probable reason the student made this error?"

3. "What did the student do right?"

4. "How can I guide the student to avoid the error in the future?"

These four questions can help to focus feedback across all grade levels and subject areas—whether you're reminding students to multiply the top number by the ones digit of the bottom or helping them recognize and respond to logical fallacies in persuasive writing.

Provide formative feedback that is specific and actionable.

You've probably experienced the frustration of receiving vague feedback—being told, for example, that a sentence in your writing is "awkward" or "clumsy" without explanation as to what was clumsy or awkward about it or how to fix it. Much more helpful, of course, is feedback that guides you toward action—for example, "Your long introductory clause makes it difficult to identify the subject of your sentence; how might you rewrite this sentence as a stronger one that leads with your subject noun?" Rather than spoon-feeding correct answers to students, the feedback you provide them during initial application should be *formative*, encouraging them to think about their learning and reflect on the process of learning. That said, feedback should also be sufficiently specific and actionable that students will know what to do with it. You're more apt to strike this balance if you (1) are clear about what error students are making, (2) can identify what students need to do differently, and (3) can identify what they should think about to improve. See Figure 4.1 for some examples.

FIGURE 4.1   EXAMPLES OF REFLECTIVE, ACTIONABLE FEEDBACK

ERROR PATTERN	WHAT STUDENTS SHOULD DO	WHAT STUDENTS SHOULD THINK ABOUT
Not supporting written claims	Expand claims with facts or details	Am I showing, not telling? Where do I need to add the word "because"?
Not lining up numbers before adding them	Align digits with the ones place	Does my answer make sense? What mistake might I have made?
Focusing on details instead of gist when summarizing text	Use headings and topic sentences to extract the gist	Where do writers put clues as to their point? What big idea do I think this writer is trying to communicate?

Help students understand and apply the "thrice is nice" principle.

You should be sure that students can perform a new skill or process three times without a mistake before turning them loose to engage in independent practice (the focus of Chapter 5). You can help students understand this pay-now-or-pay-later principle by teaching it to them and impressing upon them that learning something right the first time around will pay off later, as they can engage in fewer and shorter practice sessions yet achieve greater success. With some skills, they may develop proficiency after a handful of attempts; other skills may require a dozen or more attempts. The key is to develop proficiency during their initial guided practice session, no matter how many attempts it takes. Then, they can focus future practice on automating properly learned skills and committing new learning to long-term memory, not unlearning or relearning knowledge and skills. With this in mind, encourage your students to assess their progress honestly and ask for help during initial attempts to ensure the "cement doesn't dry," so to speak, on misconceptions or misapplications.

Shift to progress feedback as students initially master new learning.

When students are first learning new skills, they need feedback that helps them reflect on and monitor their own progress toward mastery—in essence, "going slow to go fast." You want them to, for example, fully understand every step in a problem-solving heuristic, fully internalize cognitive and metacognitive thinking strategies, and visualize what math formulas actually represent. Eventually, though, your aim is to help them automate new skills so they can free up mental bandwidth to focus on complex problem solving, critical thinking, and application of skills. In short, you actually want them to *think less* about what they're doing because they have automated and become fluent with new skills. As we'll discuss in Chapter 5, the best way to do this is through repetition, which strengthens the neural connections students are forming. As students move from guided initial application to independent practice, you can shift from formative feedback toward progress feedback, providing occasional prompts to encourage reflection when errors or mistakes occur, often with phrases that remind students of the skills they have learned but need more practice to automate (e.g., "check your work"; "show, don't tell"; "use your close-reading skills.")

Strategy 8: Peer-Assisted Consolidation of Learning

Peer-assisted consolidation of learning engages groups or pairs of students in processing, discussing, and practicing new learning.

Human beings are social creatures who crave opportunities to share our stories, experiences, and challenges with others—sometimes because we like to hear ourselves talk, but often because we want to hear what others think about our experiences. Russian psychologist Lev Vygotsky's social-constructivist theory (1978) posited that students learn primarily through social interactions with teachers, parents, and peers. This theory of socially constructed knowledge is reflected in experimental studies that, together, point to the power of *peer-assisted consolidation of learning*. We use this phrase intentionally, as opposed to the more common term "cooperative learning" (used in previous editions of *Classroom Instruction That Works*). In every study we examined, students were not *introduced* to new learning through peer-assisted learning; rather, groups were used to help them process knowledge and skills already introduced through teacher-facilitated learning. We make this point because over the years we've seen teachers use cooperative learning to introduce students to new ideas and skills—for example, pairing them up as buddies to read new texts together or turning groups of students loose to invent solutions to complex math problems. With this in mind, we have positioned this strategy as one that *follows* initial direct instruction of key concepts and skills.

Our review of research yielded nine empirical studies relating to peer-assisted learning interventions (see the Appendix) that demonstrated significant positive effect sizes (improvement index = 8–42)—across all grade levels and subject areas and with racially diverse students, multilingual learners, and students in poverty. As with other strategies, peer-assisted consolidation of learning was typically not studied as a stand-alone intervention but within an integrated bundle of strategies that often included vocabulary instruction, strategy instruction and modeling, high-level questions, and student explanations.

Guiding principles for peer-assisted consolidation of learning

The following principles for peer-assisted consolidation of learning emerge from these studies.

Peer-assisted learning should complement, not replace, direct instruction.

This point bears repeating. Across all nine studies, peer-assisted learning followed direct instruction of knowledge and skills, providing students with opportunities to pause and process what was learned through direct instruction. For example, Kim and colleagues (2017) found statistically significant effects in 3rd graders' reading comprehension (improvement index = 8) when direct instruction of basic reading skills was followed with reciprocal teaching and class debate to deepen understanding of cognitively complex fiction and nonfiction texts. Similarly, Saddler and Graham (2005) found positive effects (improvement index = 24) for an intervention that paired 4th graders to practice a sentence-combining strategy following direct instruction and modeling of the strategy. In short, peer-assisted learning should not *supplant* but rather *supplement* teacher-led instruction.

Structured activities are the key to effective peer-assisted learning.

Peer-learning activities should be structured to support student consolidation of learning—for example, providing questions to guide discussions of cognitively challenging texts (Guthrie et al., 2004) or using structured reciprocal teaching protocols to improve reading comprehension (Kim et al., 2017). There are no studies that have found positive effects for unstructured peer learning. Kramarski and Mevarech (2003), for example, compared the effects of engaging 8th grade students in four different conditions for learning to interpret graphs in mathematics: group discussions with and without teacher-provided questions to guide conversations as well as independent learning with and without teacher-provided questions. Students who engaged in peer learning with teacher-provided questions outperformed all others, including those working in unstructured groups without the benefit of structured questions (improvement index = 28). The researchers found no benefits for unstructured cooperative learning versus independent learning. In fact, students who engaged in structured *independent* learning outperformed those in unstructured groups (improvement index = 9).

Effective peer-assisted learning integrates individual accountability with positive interdependence.

Peer-assisted learning strategies should also be designed for *positive interdependence* (Johnson & Johnson, 1999), which avoids the "free rider effect" (Slavin, 1990) by holding students accountable for individual work while at the same time ensuring individual success does not come at the expense of others. Wanzek and colleagues (2014), for example, found a peer-based learning intervention to be effective in improving racially diverse high school students' social studies knowledge. Heterogenous teams of three to five students worked together to achieve consensus on comprehension-check questions and develop shared responses to high-level questions (e.g., "Consider the top three priorities for the nation as it moves from isolationism to expansionism. Then, consider the most pivotal moments in each president's term and make recommendations as to whether the same or a different course of action is required."). After each three-week unit, students held each other accountable through a peer-evaluation process in which they reflected on the contributions of individual team members to the group's success. After 20 weeks, students engaged in structured team-based learning significantly outperformed those receiving traditional instruction on measures of content knowledge (improvement index = 16) and reading comprehension (improvement index = 8). Along similar lines, a multifaceted intervention with significant effects on the reading skills (improvement index = 10) of students in high-poverty middle schools assigned students to mixed-ability teams that worked together (in pairs and small groups). Students improved their individual scores on comprehension-check quizzes, which in turn contributed to an overall team score used to determine when teams could advance to the next performance level (Stevens, 2003).

Mixed-ability groups benefit all students.

There is power in strategically designed mixed-ability groups—for example, pairing stronger writers with weaker ones to practice combining sentences (Saddler & Graham, 2005), creating mixed-ability teams to support reading and writing (Stevens, 2003), or creating heterogenous teams to improve social studies learning (Wanzek et al., 2014). Contrary to some teachers' or parents' concerns that mixed-ability groups slow the pace of learning for high-achieving students, no evidence suggests this occurs. If anything, peer-assisted learning may benefit high-achieving students more than low-achieving ones. For example, Wanzek and colleagues (2014) found that previously moderate- and high-performing students showed greater growth with team-based learning than did previously low-achieving students. One possible explanation for this difference may be that higher achieving students are better equipped to engage in dialogue with peers than students with low prior knowledge or reading skills, who may benefit more from direct instruction and scaffolding of learning—in keeping with the principle that peer-based learning should supplement, not supplant, direct instruction of key knowledge and skills.

Classroom tips for peer-assisted consolidation of learning

When properly structured and strategically designed, peer-assisted learning groups can deepen student consolidation of learning with the potential added benefit of increasing student engagement and motivation to learn. Here are some tips to help you translate these principles into effective learning experiences for your students.

"Chunk" lessons to help students pause and process learning.

Because students' brains tend to "time out" after 5 to 10 minutes of focused effort, it's important to build little "brain breaks" into your lessons by chunking them into 5- to 10-minute segments, interspersed with opportunities for students to pause and process their learning. You can use any of the strategies highlighted in this chapter during these pauses: guided application to consolidate new skills, high-level questions to reflect on learning, or peer-assisted consolidation of learning to process new learning with others. No matter how pressed you may feel for time, if you fail to provide students with these "brain breaks," they are apt to tune out—or act out. So be sure to give students (and their brains) regular opportunities to process learning.

Assign students to strategically designed mixed-ability groups.

Peer-assisted learning works best when students of different abilities, experiences, and prior knowledge come together to support each other, engaging in dialogue to contribute different perspectives and build shared understanding of new learning. Don't take the easy way out and let students determine their own groups. Not only may some students get left out, but students will also miss the rich learning opportunities that emerge in mixed-ability groups. Heterogenous groups provide opportunities for students to learn from peers and engage in self-explanation of new learning—which, as we've seen, is a powerful learning strategy. Your peer-learning groups should represent a mix of perspectives and prior knowledge. You might even design such groups as semipermanent teams that span an entire semester or school year to help students build positive interdependence with one another.

Embed high-level questions and student explanations into peer-assisted learning.

Like chocolate and peanut butter, high-level questions and peer-assisted learning pair nicely (see Guthrie et al., 2004; Kim et al., 2017; Kramarski & Mevarech,

2003; Vaughn et al., 2017; Wanzek et al., 2014). This is not surprising. For starters, small groups provide more opportunities for all students to respond to high-level questions than whole-group discussions. Also, focusing small groups on high-level questions (versus recall questions) supports consolidation of learning by helping students draw connections to prior learning and cluster learning into larger concepts, themes, and understandings. It's OK to provide small groups with some "warm-up" recall questions, but ultimately the conversation should move students to a deeper level of understanding and consolidation. Figure 4.2 provides examples of high-level questions used to structure small-group conversations for elementary, middle, and high school students.

FIGURE 4.2   HIGH-LEVEL QUESTIONS THAT CAN HELP STRUCTURE PEER-ASSISTED CONSOLIDATION OF LEARNING

QUESTION TYPE	ELEMENTARY SCHOOL	MIDDLE SCHOOL	HIGH SCHOOL
Comprehension	Who is the main character of the story? What makes you say that?	How would you describe photosynthesis as a step-by-step process?	What is the writer's main point?
Connection	How are plants similar to animals? How are they different?	How was the French revolution similar to the American revolution?	How does entropy affect weather patterns?
Strategic	What are three different ways to calculate the area of an irregular shape?	What improvements would make our model car go faster?	What's the simplest way to calculate the speed of a falling object?
Critical thinking	Why do mammals thrive in colder climates?	What would someone who disagrees with you say? What counter-argument could you offer?	Is history a story of progress or repetition? Was the fall of Rome inevitable?

Use a variety of structures to engage students in peer-assisted learning.

Although structure is the key to effective peer-assisted learning, variety and novelty are the key to re-engaging students' brains when they begin to time out (Medina, 2008). Figure 4.3 (see p. 82) offers several examples of effective ways to engage students with a variety of peer-assisted learning activities. Mixing up your approaches helps to keep peer learning from feeling tiresome or overly predictable.

FIGURE 4.3   EXAMPLES OF EFFECTIVE PEER-ASSISTED
LEARNING ACTIVITIES

ACTIVITY	HOW STUDENTS BENEFIT	THE PROCEDURE
Think-write-pair-share	Helps students reflect on, deepen, and refine their opinions	Instead of asking students to simply turn and talk, first pose a high-level question, then give them a few minutes to respond to it in writing (in journals or notebooks). Once their thoughts are on paper, they can share their responses with partners.
Numbered heads together	Promotes positive interdependence within small-group conversations	In groups of four, number students from 1 to 4. Pose a high-level question to the class and ask each group to develop a thoughtful, well-supported response. After small-group discussions conclude, return to whole-class discussion and select a number from 1 to 4, asking students from each group with that number to respond to the question. Research on this technique has found it can virtually eliminate student failure on subsequent content tests (Maheady et al., 1991).
Reciprocal teaching	Consolidates multiple students' learning and helps them grasp cognitively challenging texts	Model the key comprehension strategies of summarizing, questioning, clarifying, and predicting. Divide the class into groups, and assign each student in a group one of these four roles: • The **summarizer** reads a passage and summarizes it. (For older students, this activity may follow independent reading of an entire text, with the summarizer synthesizing key ideas from the text.) • The **questioner** poses questions designed to elicit key ideas and concepts, including inferences or how to apply new information from a text. • The **clarifier** looks for hurdles to understanding, such as unfamiliar words or pronunciations; they may also seek to clarify meaning by rereading a passage or asking for help, as necessary. • The **predictor** asks the group what they think will happen next (or what implications or applications might be drawn from the reading) and records the group's response.

Final Thoughts: Helping Students Pause, Process, and Consolidate Learning

You've probably heard students comment that something they've learned still doesn't make sense to them, or you've seen them struggle to apply a new skill successfully. What's going on in students' brains when this happens? Likely, the same thing that would happen to you if you were to, for example, take a wrong turn at a teacher conference and accidentally sit down in an investment forum. An economist walks to the podium and begins to deliver a rather dry talk about the effect of the Federal Reserve's policy of quantitative easing on interest rates and economic growth. You might feel a bit baffled by the presentation—yes, you understand the *words* the speaker is saying but cannot comprehend their meaning. As a result, you're left with a jumble of disconnected data (overnight borrowing rates, labor statistics, inflation figures) with no way to consolidate them.

What if, though, after a few minutes, the economist paused and posed a few questions for you to discuss with the person sitting next to you to develop shared understanding of what you just heard? What if you could receive some immediate feedback on your understandings? What if the whole room of investors were arranged into groups of four to engage in a friendly reciprocal teaching activity about the lecture? You might listen as someone summarized, in plain language, the gist of the talk. Another person might help clarify key terms. Another person in the small group might ask questions that help you connect what you're learning with your prior knowledge (e.g., interest rates, bank loans). Likely, things would make more sense for you.

So, when your students say that something does not make sense or they don't get how to do something, what they're really saying is that their brains need more time to pause and process their learning—often with their peers. Or they may be saying that they need some coaching—opportunities to be observed and receive feedback while trying new skills. If you can provide students with these opportunities, they will be more likely to make sense of their learning. And as a result, they'll be more prepared to engage in the next step of the learning process: moving new learning into long-term memory. In the next two chapters, we'll discuss what cognitive science reveals about these processes as well as information from experimental studies about how to support these critical phases of learning in the classroom.

5

Helping Students Practice and Reflect

When your students reach this point in the learning process (see Goodwin et al., 2020), you will have used cognitive interest cues and personal goals to help them become interested and committed to new learning. You will have helped them to focus on new learning, and they will have begun to consolidate their learning into coherent patterns to make sense of it. Yet the learning journey is far from over. In fact, it's precisely at this point that a great deal of learning often gets lost, never entering students' long-term memories. Students forget *as much as 90 percent* of what they learn in school *within a month* (Medina, 2008).

Practicing and reflecting is the fifth stage of learning. In this chapter, we'll examine some key (and surprising) principles from the science of learning that explain why so much of what students ostensibly learn never finds a home in long-term memory. We'll also identify three powerful teaching strategies you can use to improve the likelihood that students will retain what they learn in your classroom—not just for 30 days, but for a lifetime.

What the Research Says

Again, we'll start with some important insights from cognitive science, looking at how encouraging students to practice and reflect can help them transfer information from short-term working memory into long-term memory.

Repetition is key to embedding new learning in long-term memory

The first guiding principle of memory storage can be captured in three words: *repeat, repeat, repeat.* Whether a new bit of information finds a home in long-term memory depends on how often our brains return to it in order to reinforce the neural pathways used to encode the learning. Basically, if we want to retain new learning, we must go on more than one date with it, so to speak. As we described in Chapter 4, memories aren't tucked neatly away in a single neuron or tidy mental filing system; they're splattered across a messy network of neurons linked by neural pathways. *Returning* to a new memory reactivates the pathways connecting those neurons. As pathways are reactivated, the brain begins to wrap a sheath of insulation (called myelin) around them. Much like insulation around an electrical wire that helps electrical charges move more quickly, the myelin coating makes it easier for those neurons to fire together again. Hence, repetition is the key to long-term memory—for example, students must rehearse a new skill at least 24 times before they reach 80 percent competency (Anderson, 1995).

Spaced repetition strengthens memory

Scientific experiments dating back more than a century (e.g., Ebbinghaus, 1885/1964) have shown that although repetition is key to memory, the best way to encode learning into long-term memory is to space repetitions over a period of days or weeks. The age-old practice of cramming—repeating something over and again in a single practice session—may be the best way to learn something in the short term yet the *worst* way to retain it in the long term. Simply stated, cramming leads to *fast learning* and *fast forgetting.* During an all-night cram session, students might believe they've learned something because they can quickly retrieve it, yet they haven't actually stored it in long-term memory (Bjork & Bjork, 2011); this creates an "illusion of knowing" (Brown et al., 2014). Students may *think* their new learning is etched in stone, but it's really written in sand, waiting to be washed away. On the other hand, returning to new information a few days later (and again a few days after that) reinforces the existing neural pathways that formed the memory and creates additional pathways to it, which provides more ways to retrieve it.

Retrieval practice helps commit new learning to memory

A century ago, researchers made an accidental yet remarkable discovery while seeking to chart the so-called "forgetting curve"—the rate at which new information fades from memory (Gates, 1917). Quizzing subjects to see how much previously learned material they could recall revealed that incessant quizzes were "contaminating" the research. The more frequently they asked study participants to recall a particular topic, the more likely participants were to remember it. And so it was that researchers stumbled onto a powerful idea that a century later has strangely yet to become a bedrock teaching strategy: if you want to remember something, quiz yourself on it. As it turns out, racking one's brain to remember something reactivates the neural networks that were used to store the memory, which in turn wraps more myelin around those neural pathways, making the information easier to retrieve next time. It's more effective than simply rehashing, rereading, or reviewing prior learning (Brown et al., 2014). This *retrieval practice* is one of the most powerful ways to commit new learning to memory for students of all ages, from preschool (Fritz et al., 2007) through elementary school (Karpicke et al., 2016), middle school (McDaniel et al., 2011), high school (McDermott et al., 2014), and college (Karpicke & Blunt, 2011).

Mixing up practice makes learning initially more difficult but ultimately more effective

Years ago, Kerr and Booth (1978) made a fascinating discovery in an experiment with a group of several dozen 8- and 12-year-old children. Half of the group practiced tossing beanbags into a bucket at the same distance: three feet. The other half practiced at alternating distances of two and four feet. After 12 weeks, the groups competed to see how many bags they could toss into buckets placed at just a single distance: three feet. Students who had practiced from *alternating* distances were more accurate than those who practiced only at a distance of three feet—despite having never practiced tossing the bags from that distance. Why should that be? By mixing up their practice, the second group developed a better, more nuanced feel for the activity—figuring out the best arc, velocity, and hand movement for tossing the beanbag at both distances, which improved their skill at any distance.

Subsequent research has found that this same principle—*interleaving practice*—applies to academic learning. Initially, learning appears to be slower with interleaving practice, yet it grows stronger over time versus practicing just one skill or set of knowledge at a time (Rohrer & Pashler, 2010). For example, Taylor and Rohrer (2010) randomly assigned 4th graders learning how to calculate the number of faces, edges, corners, and angles of prisms to two different practice conditions. Half engaged in a traditional "block practice" session (working the same type of problem before moving onto the next); the other half engaged in interleaved practice, working different types of problems in mixed fashion. On an initial test one day later, students in the block-practice group outperformed those in the interleaved-practice group, recalling nearly 100 percent of the learning versus just 70 percent. Yet when tested again two days later, the interleaved-practice group outperformed the block practice group, retaining *even more learning* than the day before—close to 80 percent of their learning (versus less than 40 percent for the blocked-practice group). Perhaps most important, students in the interleaved practice group committed fewer "discrimination errors" in which they mistook one type of problem for another.

In short, mixing up the skills students are practicing forces their brains to work harder, making microadjustments and reflecting more deeply on what they're practicing. For example, if they must solve different types of math problems during a single practice session, they need to consider what strategy to use to divide fractions, multiply decimals, or add fractions (or calculate prism angles, edges, and faces). As it turns out, embedding such "desirable difficulties" (Bjork & Bjork, 1992) into practice sessions forces students to develop richer neural pathways to their learning, which in turn helps them to better recognize problems and adjust their problem-solving strategies when confronted with a real-world mix of problem types.

There are three evidence-based teaching strategies that can help you translate these guiding principles into independent practice opportunities that effectively employ repetition, retrieval, and reflection to help students transfer new learning into long-term memory.

Strategy 9: Retrieval Practice ("Quizzing to Remember")

Retrieval practice supports retention of new declarative knowledge by compelling students to recall new learning.

Since the days of Socrates, quizzing students has been a common fixture of teaching. Yet teachers tend to use quizzes to measure rather than to support learning—to generate yet another datapoint for their gradebooks. Or they may use the possibility of quizzes to motivate students, keeping them on their toes in anticipation of the dreaded pop quiz. Cognitive science, however, suggests that quizzing students serves an altogether different, and more powerful, purpose: helping students encode new learning into their long-term memories. Quizzing forces students to search their memories for recently encoded information and, in so doing, strengthens the newly formed neural connections to that information, thereby increasing their ability to recall it later.

Our review of research yielded 11 empirical studies that demonstrated significant positive effect sizes (improvement index = 11–37) for engaging students in retrieval practice (i.e., quizzing to remember) across a variety of subject areas, all grade levels, and student populations (see the Appendix). It's worth noting that the interventions examined in these studies were specifically designed to improve students' ability to retain and recall facts and concepts, not to engage in critical thinking or complex problem solving. The point here is not to engage students in superficial "drill-and-kill" learning but to use quizzing to build the foundational knowledge and skills students need to engage in more complex and challenging learning tasks (see Chapter 6).

Guiding principles for retrieval practice (quizzing to remember)

Here are the guiding principles for retrieval practice that emerge from these studies.

Retrieval practice is more effective than most other forms of studying.

Numerous studies demonstrate that retrieval practice is better than other more common forms of studying, such as reviewing test questions and answers (Carpenter et al., 2009), rereading texts and reviewing information (Karpicke & Blunt, 2011; Karpicke & Smith, 2012), and constructing concept maps of new learning (Karpicke & Blunt, 2011). Karpicke and Blunt (2011), for example, found large effects (improvement index = 25) for college students who engaged in retrieval practice versus those who simply reviewed the text. A similar study (Karpicke & Blunt, 2011) found that 101 of 120 students (84 percent) who engaged in retrieval practice outperformed those who constructed concept maps—even on test items that required them to construct concept maps (improvement index = 35). It's likely that retrieval practice works better than other forms of studying because it requires students to actively build a mental retrieval structure, thereby developing more retrieval cues than simply rereading, reviewing, or making concept maps.

Retrieval practice works best when students receive timely correct-answer feedback.

Studies show that retrieval practice works best when students receive correct-answer feedback shortly after making their own guesses—for example, learning the correct answer to history questions (Carpenter et al., 2009) or seeing the correct solutions to math problems (Outhwaite et al., 2019; Powell et al., 2009). This is likely because the "aha" moment that comes with a correct answer helps students reinforce the neural pathways they are creating in their minds to retrieve learning. At the same time, awaiting a correct answer creates a brief episode of curiosity, which makes students more likely to retain information (Gruber et al., 2014). So, when you quiz students and provide correct answers after a brief delay, you pique their curiosity and, in so doing, prime their brains to create long-term memories. The operative word here, though, is *brief.* If you leave students hanging too long (e.g., until the next day), their curiosity will wane along with the benefits of retrieval practice.

Speeded retrieval practice supports basic fluency but not more complex skills.

A handful of studies have demonstrated significant positive effects for speeded or timed retrieval practice. For example, Dyson and colleagues (2015) engaged low-achieving, low-income kindergartners in speeded retrieval practice with simple math flash cards. Encouraging students to recall as many correct answers as they could in a limited time delivered nearly twice the learning gains (improvement index = 29) as engaging them in an untimed, slow-paced number-line game designed to develop the same skills. Other researchers found that engaging at-risk 4th graders in solving as many basic fraction problems as possible during five-minute "sprints" demonstrated significantly greater gains on multiple measures of math problem solving (improvement index = 23–37) than having students spend the same amount of time using math manipulatives to explain their solutions to fractions problems (Fuchs et al., 2014).

Such findings may surprise some educators, who may have been told that flash cards and speeded practice put undue pressure on kids or result in superficial learning. The reality is more nuanced. Speeded retrieval practice can help students build basic skills and need not be high-pressure, especially when framed as a learning game or as a competition against oneself, not others. After all, many students thoroughly enjoy *subjecting themselves* to a form of speeded practice called video games. That said, it's worth noting that retrieval practice alone seldom transfers to complex problem-solving skills, as Fuchs and colleagues (2009) found when comparing the effects of 16 weeks of retrieval practice with flash cards versus 16 weeks of tutoring in word problem-solving skills. Flash card practice boosted student fluency with math skills (improvement index = 21) over a nonpractice control group, but these gains did not transfer to word problem-solving skills. In sum, flash cards and timed practice can help students develop fluency with essential basic knowledge and skills, but do not confuse these skills with deeper learning. Stated differently, think of speeded retrieval practice as necessary, but not sufficient, for deeper learning.

Retrieval practice should support initial mastery and then be repeated in spaced intervals.

As noted in Chapter 4, the goal of initial practice sessions is for students to retrieve new learning properly at least three times (Rawson & Dunlosky, 2011). Karpicke and Smith (2012) illustrated the importance of achieving mastery during initial practice sessions when they gave students a list of 30 words to memorize. Some students were encouraged to drop words from further practice as soon as they felt they could recall them; however, these students significantly underperformed those instructed to engage in multiple rounds of retrieval practice for every word on the list. It is likely that for students in the first group, words began to look familiar after a couple of exposures, which prompted them to drop words too quickly, before actually learning them. Ample evidence also points to the need to spread retrieval practice sessions over days and even weeks. Positive effects have been reported, for example, for providing kindergartners with 24 half-hour practice sessions (Dyson et al., 2015), 3rd graders with retrieval practice opportunities three times a week for 16 weeks (e.g., Fuchs et al., 2009), and using a math app to support 4- and 5-year-olds with 12 weeks of play-based retrieval practice (Outhwaite et al., 2019). In short, multiple practice sessions spread over time appear to be the key to helping students develop the strong neural connections they need to embed new learning in long-term memory.

Classroom tips for retrieval practice

"Quizzing to remember"—that is, giving students opportunities to rack their brains to recall new learning—strengthens freshly formed neural networks. Remember, though, that the point of retrieval practice is *not* to simply engage in "drill-and-kill" learning. Rather, the goal is to help students automate basic knowledge and skills needed to engage in the kinds of complex problem solving, critical thinking, and inquiry-based learning we'll explore in Chapter 6. These classroom tips can help you to translate these principles into effective retrieval practice opportunities for your students.

Quiz more, grade less.

Perhaps the most important thing to consider when quizzing to remember is you don't need to grade all of these quizzes. Seriously. After all, the purpose of retrieval practice is to support—not measure—learning. If you're worried students won't take the quizzes seriously if you're not grading them, help them to understand that quizzes are meant to serve as *practice* opportunities for sharpening their minds. As with other endeavors, it's important to practice well in order to perform well. Do coaches grade players during basketball practice? Do band instructors grade students practicing at home? No. Yet students work hard at both, especially if they aspire to win the next game or perform well in front of an audience. Retrieval practice serves the same purpose—it strengthens students' brains and memories so they can achieve their learning goals. You can continue to provide students with all sorts of quizzes—as bell-ringer activities and spontaneous mid-lesson checks for understanding—while disabusing yourself of the idea that you need to fill your gradebook with scores on all of those quizzes.

Provide students with timely correct-answer feedback on quizzes.

Don't leave students hanging for correct answers after quizzing them to remember. Too often (especially when quizzes are intended as fodder for gradebooks) students might wait 24 hours or longer before they see the correct answers to a quiz. This not only robs them of the curiosity that can support retention of new learning but also deprives them of the "aha" moments that can strengthen their developing neural networks. Immediately after each quiz, provide students with the correct answers, giving them opportunities to correct their work and ask questions to clarify misunderstandings.

Balance speeded practice for basic skills with reflective practice for complex skills.

As we've mentioned, speeded practice can support fluency and automaticity of the basic skills needed to engage in more complex problem solving. It's difficult for students to solve complex math problems if they cannot readily retrieve math basic facts, to engage in spirited classroom debate if they do not understand essential vocabulary, or to converse in a foreign language if they stumble over verb conjugations. In short, speeded practice has its place in the classroom. So, once students have achieved basic conceptual understanding and comprehension (i.e., they can *make sense of learning*), identify the knowledge and skills they must automate and provide students with speeded practice opportunities to develop fluency. That said, be sure to balance speeded practice with reflective practice that gives students opportunities to slow down and reflect on what might be missing or misunderstood with self-evaluative check-ins (e.g., "One thing that doesn't make sense to me is . . ." or "One thing I can't seem to figure out is . . .").

Strategy 10: Spaced, Mixed Independent Practice

Spaced, mixed independent practice sessions support long-term memory through repeated encounters, spaced over days and weeks, that engage students in a mix of problem types and knowledge.

If you were in a traditional classroom as a student, you likely encountered a fairly predictable cadence of learning. You read a text at home, and your teacher lectured on it the following day. Or perhaps your teacher would demonstrate a new skill in class and, if you were lucky, would circulate the room observing you and your classmates, offering some guidance during your initial attempts to master new skills. Afterward, you and your classmates would likely practice problems 1 through 25 from the book at home, which you might discuss the next day in class (or just submit for a grade). After that, the class would move on to the next bit of learning, never to return again to the problems or concepts covered—except for maybe on a stray quiz here and there. At best, your teacher might touch lightly on the new knowledge and skills in a review session prior to the unit test. After the unit test, the class would move on to new learning, never to return again to what you had learned—with the possible exception of an end-of-term final.

Unfortunately, this "teach once, practice once, test once" cadence of learning is still far too common, yet research shows it is far from best practice because it doesn't reflect how the brain works. The brain retains new information only after several encounters with it—multiple opportunities to think about, retrieve and recall, and practice new learning—and ideally, while practicing a variety of skills during the same session. Thus, to help students embed learning in long-term memory, you need to provide them with multiple opportunities, spread over days and weeks, to practice a mix of new skills and learning.

We identified seven empirical studies with significant positive effects (improvement index = 9 to 47) for engaging diverse learners in spaced and mixed practice opportunities (see the Appendix). Although the interventions examined in these studies focused on developing students' math skills, the same science-of-learning principle of repetition over time applies to helping students develop skills in other areas—such as writing, balancing science equations, or developing athletic or artistic talents.

Guiding principles for spaced, mixed independent practice

The following guiding principles for providing students with interleaved and spaced independent practice emerge from these studies.

Massed practice leads to fast learning—and fast forgetting.

Caffeine-fueled late-night cram sessions may be a time-honored tradition among students, but as we've seen, it's an ineffective learning strategy. As two cognitive scientists who studied the effects of cramming concluded, "procedures that produce fast learning can produce fast forgetting" (Roediger & Pyc, 2012, p. 244). So, the first key principle to emerge from research is that to form strong, lasting memories, practice opportunities should be spread over days and even weeks, not crammed in the night before the test.

Interleaving practice problems supports greater retention of learning.

Another common (yet ineffective) approach to learning is engaging students in *blocked practice*, solving similar problems that all require the same procedures during the same practice session (e.g., "carrying the 10" in two-column addition). It's more beneficial to present students with a mix of problems that require them to first identify the problem type and then access the appropriate problem-solving strategy. Empirical studies support this conclusion. Mayfield and Chase (2002) found that, among college students learning algebra rules, those who engaged in massed practice (i.e., answering 50 questions on a single rule they had just learned) significantly underperformed those who engaged in interleaved practice (i.e., answering 50 questions that covered a mix of rules covered in prior learning). The difference between these two groups was significant on both measures of application (improvement index = 47) and general algebra skills (improvement index = 35). Similar positive effects for interleaved practice were reported in three other experimental studies (improvement index = 22 to 35; Rohrer et al., 2014, 2020; Woodward, 2006).

Students may initially feel frustrated with interleaving practice, as it can appear to "slow down" their learning. Traditional blocked practice does, in fact, support better initial gains in learning, especially when students are tested on the same items they practiced. Yet over time, those who engage in interleaving practice catch up to and surpass students engaged in blocked practice, especially when tested on a mix of problem types (which is more reflective of real-world experience). In essence, interleaving practice helps students "go slow to go fast" by developing richer neural connections with new learning and, thus, better retention and retrieval.

Mixing up the presentation of problems also supports greater retention of learning.

A similar principle applies to how you present practice problems to students; mixing up the format may slow down initial gains in learning but it supports greater long-term retention. For example, in an experiment with 3rd grade students, McNeil and colleagues (2011) provided one group of students with extra practice problems presented in a nontraditional format (e.g., $17 = 9 + 8$), a second group with extra practice problems presented in a traditional format (e.g., $9 + 8 = 17$), and a third group with no extra practice problems. On a subsequent post-test of equation-solving abilities, students who practiced with nontraditional problems significantly outperformed those who practiced with traditional problems (improvement index = 28). Similar findings emerged in a study with 2nd grade students (Powell et al., 2015); students exposed to a mix of problems presented in traditional and nontraditional formats significantly outperformed those presented with problems in a traditional format on measures of their problem-solving skills (improvement index = 24). Switching up the format of problems creates the sort of "desirable difficulties" that cognitive scientists have determined help students think more deeply about the problems they are solving and, thus, more richly encode the related learning into long-term memory (Bjork & Bjork, 1992).

Following a 3x3 schedule for independent practice enhances retention of new learning.

Initial practice sessions, when we want students to achieve repeated mastery with new learning at least three times, should be followed by at least two more practice sessions. In an analysis of 335 college students' learning during multiple practice sessions, achieving initial mastery (i.e., correctly recalling a single study item three times) required an average of 6.3 minutes of practice time per item (Rawson & Dunlosky, 2011). Two more practice sessions required an additional 2.7 minutes of practice time per item but yielded 62 percent gains in overall performance. Adding a fourth and fifth practice session further improved performance, but with diminishing returns, leading Rawson and Dunlosky (2011) to conclude that optimal practice reflects a 3x3 schedule—practicing to three correct recalls during an initial session followed by two subsequent learning sessions.

Classroom tips for spaced, mixed independent practice

Collectively, these studies demonstrate the power of engaging students in multiple practice opportunities spread over days and weeks. They also demonstrate the importance of helping students "go slow to go fast" by presenting "desirable difficulties" during practice sessions—engaging them in solving a mix of problems and problems presented in different formats, which compels them to think more deeply about the problems they are solving. Together, these strategies help students maximize practice sessions, building the neural connections needed to ensure long-term storage and retrieval of learning. We offer the following classroom tips to help you effectively incorporate interleaved, spaced practice into student learning experiences.

Build spaced practice opportunities into unit plans.

As you design learning units, list all of the knowledge and skills you want students to develop. Next, build in *at least three* opportunities for students to practice both the declarative and the procedural knowledge they should commit to long-term memory. For many teachers (and textbooks), this can be a departure from current lesson and unit design, which often follows a format that looks something like this:

- I teach X. Students practice X.
- I teach Y. Students practice Y.
- I teach Z. Students practice Z.
- Finally, I test students on X, Y, and Z.

Because one-off practice sessions are ineffective, you must build multiple opportunities, spaced over time, for students to practice new knowledge and skills. How exactly can you do that? Fortunately, the concept of interleaving practice points to an answer.

Mix up repeated practice opportunities.

After initial guided application (e.g., a focus on a teaching a single strategy for solving a specific type of math problem), you can weave prior learning into subsequent practice sessions—for example, engage students in solving problems, recalling vocabulary, and practicing skills they learned during a prior lesson or unit. Figure 5.1 illustrates how you might integrate these first two tips to provide interleaved, cumulative practice opportunities that engage students in practicing new skills while also allowing them to rehearse prior knowledge and skills at least three times over the course of a unit.

FIGURE 5.1   A SCHEDULE FOR INTERLEAVING AND SPACED PRACTICE OPPORTUNITIES

SKILL	PRACTICE SESSION 1	PRACTICE SESSION 2	PRACTICE SESSION 3	PRACTICE SESSION 4	PRACTICE SESSION 5
New skill to be mastered: Conjugating regular Spanish verbs (*beber, comer, correr*) in preterit tense	x		x		x
New skill to be mastered: Conjugating irregular verbs (*tener, venir, hacer*) in preterit tense		x		x	x
Prior skill to be reviewed: Conjugating regular Spanish verbs (*beber, comer, correr*) in present tense		x		x	
Prior skill to be reviewed: Conjugating irregular verbs (*tener, venir, hacer*) in present tense	x		x		

Mix up the format and presentation of problems.

You can also help students develop more robust neural connections to new learning by mixing up how you present problems—for example, switching the presentation of equations (e.g., $13 = 7 + 3x$ instead of $7 + 3x = 13$) or changing conjugation tables so that third-person plural is in the upper-left corner (instead of lower-right). These little tweaks create "desirable difficulties" that prompt students to think more deeply about what they're practicing and, as a result, develop more and deeper "hooks" for retrieving knowledge. This is especially valuable when students face novel problems or problems framed slightly differently than how they initially learned them—and again, this is more like real-world settings. Rarely do adults encounter only two-column multiplication problems all day or speak solely in third-person preterit tense all day.

Teach and encourage the 3x3 schedule for independent practice.
As students reread texts or their class notes, it's easy for them to believe that they've committed new learning to memory. But when put to the test (literally), they realize they have not retained or cannot retrieve what they've learned. You can help students avoid this pitfall by teaching them to adopt the 3x3 schedule for independent practice. Older or more successful learners may be able to write their own questions. Others may benefit from questions you provide for this purpose. Returning to the tip in Chapter 4, teach them the "thrice is nice" rule during initial learning: if they can correctly recall new learning three times, then they can move on.

The second and equally important part of the 3x3 schedule is engaging in at least two more practice sessions. This is most likely not common practice for many students, who may at best engage in just a single study or practice session prior to a test. However, three practice sessions can lead to more than 60 percent improvement in performance. In other words, you should teach the 3x3 schedule to students, but don't assume they will follow it without some direction (i.e., assigned practice sessions spread over a week or two).

Strategy 11: Targeted Support (Scaffolded Practice)

Targeted support provides students at risk of failure with intensive strategy instruction, guided practice, and formative feedback to enhance conceptual understanding, procedural fluency, and consolidation of learning.

Despite your best efforts to deliver effective and engaging learning experiences, there will be times when some students will not master new learning. When this occurs, you need to provide them with additional support and practice opportunities—often in a more targeted and scaffolded way. You might need to help them focus on new learning in a different way, observe them more closely to see what misconceptions they have or which mistakes they are making, or provide them with tailored feedback to support their success. Simply stated, you need to catch them before they fall. In many classrooms, especially those following a multitiered system of supports or response to invention model, such supports are commonly referred to as Tier 2 instruction—supplemental teaching designed to augment Tier 1 (i.e., "best first") instruction. A large body of evidence builds a strong case for supporting students in small groups with additional concentrated learning cycles that repeat prior phases of learning and employ evidence-based practices.

We've labeled these concentrated learning cycles "targeted supports" to convey that they should be temporary and focused on specific student learning needs (rather than considering or referring to students as "Tier 2 kids"—a cringeworthy moniker educators sometimes apply). It is not unusual to find that a handful of students need additional support on a particular unit but not on the next. In short, when properly implemented, targeted supports should be short-lived, precisely because they helped students achieve mastery and are no longer necessary.

We identified 18 studies reporting significant effects (improvement index = 16 to 38) for interventions that provided small-group, scaffolded practice opportunities to students identified as being at risk of learning failure (see the Appendix). Although most of these studies focused on improving reading and math skills among elementary students, it is reasonable to assume that providing students who struggle during initial learning with additional opportunities to achieve mastery would yield positive benefits for older students and in other subject areas.

Guiding principles for targeted support

The following guiding principles for providing students with targeted support and scaffolded practice emerge from these studies.

Targeted support can close achievement gaps.

The high effect sizes across these studies are noteworthy because, in many cases, they resulted from interventions for students who had previously been identified with significant learning gaps in reading or math. In some cases, targeted supports helped students to practically catch up with higher performing peers. For example, Coyne and colleagues (2019) compared the effects of supplementing 20 minutes of daily whole-class (Tier 1) vocabulary instruction with 30 minutes of small-group (Tier 2) vocabulary intervention for racially diverse kindergartners at risk for language and learning difficulties. After 22 weeks of intervention, students receiving Tier 2 supports demonstrated significant gains over students receiving Tier 1 instruction only (improvement index = 36)—so much so that previously low-performing students demonstrated grade-level learning on these measures.

As Coyne and colleagues observed, the treatment, in effect, counteracted the pernicious "Matthew effects" (see Merton, 1968) of capable readers making more rapid gains in vocabulary knowledge and reading skills than less capable ones. Similarly, Connor and colleagues (2011) studied the effects of a software-based intervention that tracked 1st grade students' vocabulary and reading development and offered teachers individualized instructional guidance to improve student outcomes. Over the course of a school year, compared with students in the control group, those in the treatment group demonstrated significant gains in reading skills (improvement index = 19)—equivalent to two additional months of learning. Even greater effects (improvement index = 22) emerged for students whose initial reading and vocabulary scores were below the 25th percentile—in effect, closing the learning gap with their previously higher performing peers.

Formative assessment data is key to targeting learning supports.

Supports and scaffolding are most effective when they are *targeted to student learning needs,* using formative assessment data to identify which students need support and what supports they need (Connor et al., 2011, 2013; Coyne et al., 2019; Vaughn et al., 2006). In several studies (Coyne et al., 2019; Fuchs et al., 2013; Vaughn et al., 2006), students receiving targeted supports were initially identified for intervention based on prior achievement (e.g., English learners who tested below the 25th percentile in language proficiency). Students made significant learning gains (improvement index = 16 to 36) after receiving supplemental targeted instruction in the skills they had yet to learn (e.g., phonemic awareness, letter knowledge, word recognition, connected text fluency, comprehension strategies). Two separate studies (Connor et al., 2011, 2013) found significant short- and long-term effects for a software-based intervention that tracked students' vocabulary and reading skills and recommend targeted reading instruction for individual students (improvement index = 19 and 17, respectively). Basically, the point is that data should focus supplemental teaching and learning where it is most needed, measure student progress toward mastery, and identify when additional supports are no longer necessary.

Supports are most effective when structured and delivered by trained professionals.

Across multiple studies, targeted supports were typically delivered by skilled professionals who followed structured protocols for supporting student learning (Connor et al., 2013; Coyne et al., 2019; Fuchs, Geary et al., 2013; Fuchs,

Schumacher, et al., 2013; Nelson et al., 2011; Vadasy & Sanders, 2008, 2010). Fuchs, Schumacher, and colleagues (2013) studied the effects of engaging at-risk 4th grade students in scripted small-group (3:1 ratio) tutoring. These lessons sought to develop students' conceptual understanding of fractions, develop automaticity with foundational skills, and promote self-regulation. Small-group tutoring sessions followed a structured sequence of teaching and learning activities that included helping students visualize mathematics concepts with number lines, circles, and manipulatives; direct instruction of academic vocabulary; strategy instruction and modeling; and spaced retrieval practice to develop automaticity. Students in the treatment group significantly outperformed (improvement index = 24) those in the control group, who received whole-class instruction only.

Similarly, Nelson and colleagues (2011) found significant positive effects for providing Tier 2 vocabulary instruction to racially diverse, low-income students with a structured phonics-based instruction protocol, which included direct instruction in word blending and meaning, fast reading of short passages to reinforce decoding skills, and providing students with "say a sentence" practice opportunities to reinforce understanding of target words. Students in the control group, meanwhile, engaged in a less structured version of Tier 2 vocabulary development—a modified form of interactive book reading in which tutors used picture cards to introduce new words to students prior to reading, asked open-ended questions to develop word knowledge during reading, and encouraged students to practice target words after reading. On a post-test, students in the structured treatment group significantly outperformed those in the loosely structured control group on measures of vocabulary knowledge (improvement index = 35) and word reading skills (improvement index = 25).

A key takeaway from these studies is that to be effective, targeted supports should not be ad hoc or loosely scripted reviews of prior learning but rather structured "minilessons" that target student needs and engage them in concentrated cycles of learning. It's worth noting that across multiple studies, effective targeted supports were delivered by trained professionals (i.e., teachers, interventionists, paraprofessionals) who understood both what students needed to learn and how to teach it.

Targeted support should supplement, not supplant, best first instruction.
Although many studies have reported significant effect sizes for targeted supports versus whole-class instruction alone (Connor et al., 2011; Coyne et al., 2019; Fuchs, Schumacher et al., 2013; Vadasy & Sanders, 2008), these same

studies suggest that even well-delivered targeted supports cannot overcome ineffective classroom instruction. For starters, many of the interventions in our sample were designed to supplement Tier 1 instruction (Coyne et al., 2019; Dyson et al., 2015; Nelson et al., 2011; Vaughn et al., 2006). Moreover, Tier 2 interventions appeared to be only as effective as the Tier 1 instruction they supported. For instance, a study of an 18-week daily pull-out phonics tutoring session for multilingual and English-only kindergartners found overall positive effects for the intervention (improvement index = 30; Vadasy & Sanders, 2010). Yet for students in classrooms with low-quality instruction, tutoring served to enhance their basic skills (e.g., spelling) but did not support gains in more advanced skills (e.g., reading comprehension). Meanwhile, for students in classrooms with high-quality instruction, tutoring significantly improved both their basic and advanced skills.

Classroom tips for targeted support

Collectively, these studies demonstrate the power of providing students with additional opportunities to acquire, process, and practice learning they initially struggle to master. Targeted supports do not simply repeat initial learning experiences (akin to Albert Einstein's definition of insanity of doing the same thing yet expecting different results). Rather, they help students "go slow to go fast" by providing them with more intentional and methodical opportunities to focus on new learning, often in a different way, such as using manipulatives to develop conceptual understanding of math problems or making new, personal connections to academic vocabulary. Targeted support also includes providing opportunities for students to practice learning, often under the watchful eye of a tutor who can provide formative feedback that helps students correct their mistakes and misunderstandings. With this in mind, we offer the following tips for providing your students with effective targeted supports and scaffolded practice opportunities.

Ensure Tier 1 instruction provides opportunities to master key knowledge and skills.

Targeted supports are only necessary when initial (Tier 1) instruction fails to help students achieve mastery. In other words, the more effective Tier 1 instruction is, the fewer students will require additional support. So, as you plan each unit of instruction, carefully identify the foundational knowledge and skills your students must master. Be clear about what success will look like for your students (set those success criteria!), and ensure you plan for and deliver well-structured opportunities for students to focus on new learning, make sense of their learning, and practice the new learning. Targeted supports are, after all, time-intensive for both you and your students; your goal in providing initial instruction should be to help as many students as possible (ideally, all of them) grasp new learning the first time around to avoid the need for targeted supports.

Use regular checks during independent practice to catch students before they fall.

As students engage in independent practice, use regular quizzes (i.e., retrieval practice), classroom observations, and practice assignments to track each student's progress toward mastery. This will help you to readily identify those who might be struggling to master new learning. Learning difficulties are often easy to solve when diagnosed early and more difficult to alleviate when diagnosed late. You don't want to wait until an end-of-unit test to realize students are struggling. Rather, you want to identify their struggles early so you can provide them with what can often be simple and brief targeted supports to get them back on track.

Structure targeted supports as mini learning cycles.

The most effective targeted supports aren't ad hoc or loosely structured review sessions; rather, they are structured learning opportunities that deliver a concentrated cycle of relearning (see Figure 5.2). Typically, you'll start with reteaching key knowledge or skills students are struggling to master, explaining the concept or demonstrating the skill in a different way (e.g., more visual or deconstructed). For example, you might use manipulatives or concrete examples to explain a concept or break a process down into its component parts and systematically model each step of the process. Next, give students an opportunity to retry the learning. As they do, observe them closely to see what mistakes they may be making or misconceptions they may harbor. Then provide them with many opportunities to practice their learning and receive formative feedback to correct their mistakes and misconceptions.

Offer targeted supports to small groups while others engage in independent practice.

Several studies have found positive effects for providing targeted supports to students in small groups (e.g., three to five students); there appears to be no particular benefit to tutoring students as individuals versus in pairs (Vadasy & Sanders, 2008). In short, you can comfortably provide supplemental

FIGURE 5.2   THE TARGETED SUPPORT CYCLE

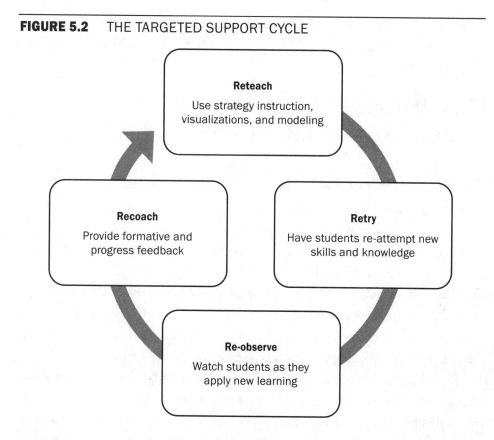

instruction to students in small groups. So, what should other students do while you (or a paraprofessional) deliver targeted supports? Independent practice. Remember: all students benefit from multiple, spaced (and interleaved) practice opportunities; while you provide targeted supports to some students, others can practice prior learning, including knowledge and skills they may have previously learned but which are not yet fully embedded in their long-term memories.

Use data to determine (and celebrate) when students no longer need targeted supports.

As noted earlier, Tier 2 small groups should not be considered permanent, nor should students be identified as "Tier 2 kids." If targeted supports are designed and delivered well, they ought to catch students up so that they don't require additional supplemental instruction. The only way to know that for sure, of course, is to continue to track their progress and have students monitor their own progress as well, so that you (and they) know when extra support is no longer needed. When this happens, be sure to congratulate students on their progress. This helps them connect their extra efforts with their success and, in so doing, reinforces a growth mindset by attributing positive outcomes to their hard work.

Final Thoughts: Helping Students Repeat to Remember

Repetition is the key to memory, in keeping with the well-worn adage that practice makes perfect. Yet *how* students engage in practice is the true key to memory—in keeping with another well-worn adage that *perfect* practice makes perfect. Basically, the number of hours students spend practicing is less important than what they do during those hours—something we uncovered a decade ago in our meta-analysis for the second edition of this book when we found that the effect size for practice was *four times greater* than the effect size for homework (Beesley & Apthorp, 2010). In short, the key to student success has never been to pile on the homework but rather to give students well-structured (i.e., spaced and mixed) opportunities to practice their learning.

In a departure from the two previous versions of *Classroom Instruction That Works,* which called out "homework and practice" as a category of effective instruction, we've dropped the word "homework" from this version in favor of referring to specific types of practice. In making this change, we are not necessarily arguing that homework is bad or that teachers shouldn't assign it. Rather, our point is that homework assignments ought to be intentional and serve a purpose, such as providing students with opportunities to engage in independent, interleaved, and spaced practice or (as we'll explore in Chapter 6) to engage in opportunities to extend and apply their learning.

That said, if homework *is* practice, what's the purpose of grading such assignments? Grading homework might send the message that practice assignments are yet another perfunctory hoop students must jump through in order to accumulate a desired score in a teacher's gradebook. Instead, we want to encourage students to be *deliberate* in their practice, reflecting on their progress, identifying gaps in performance, and focusing on knowledge and skills they still need to refine.

Finally, it bears repeating that practicing new skills to develop automaticity and fluency is not the final destination of learning. Yes, rote learning has a place in learning, inasmuch as it helps students to automate foundational skills and knowledge so they can engage in more complex learning. Hence, practice (even *perfect* practice) supports a rather limited and superficial form of learning—which is necessary but not sufficient for deep learning. In the next chapter, we'll explore how you can help students extend and apply what they've learned during the previous five phases of learning to engage in deeper, more lasting, and meaningful learning.

6

Helping Students Extend and Apply Learning

Embedding discrete concepts and skills in long-term memory (what we might call "book smarts") is valuable, but it's only part of what it means to be educated. Most would agree that it is what we can *do* with our learning that's more important—whether it's doctors translating their formal education into the skills needed to diagnose and cure illnesses, plumbers applying their technical training to fix leaking pipes, or teachers applying and adapting their formal education and professional learning (and books like this!) into effective learning experiences for students. In short, being able to use knowledge to think through and solve real-world problems (what we might call "know-how") is arguably the true essence of what it means to be educated, especially if the aim isn't simply to prepare students for trivia night at the pub but to help them better understand the world and take informed action that leads to positive outcomes for themselves and others.

However, students are unlikely to develop know-how if all they ever do in school is regurgitate information on a test. As we'll discuss in this chapter, they need opportunities to *extend and apply* their learning by engaging in mentally challenging writing exercises, investigating complex phenomena, and solving complex problems.

What the Research Says

Let's start with what happens in students' minds when they extend and apply their learning through cognitively challenging tasks.

Mental models are the key to deep learning

Years ago, researchers discovered an interesting principle of memory forma-tion when they examined the ability of chess grand masters to quickly memo-rize the location of every piece on a chessboard—until those pieces were placed *randomly* instead of as the result of gameplay. Suddenly, the grand masters were no better than novice chess players at memorizing the location of pieces on the board. As it turns out, the grand masters didn't have photographic memories, but rather a well-honed ability to see patterns resulting from moves—a skill developed from thousands of hours of playing chess (de Groot, 1966). In short, they had mental models, or *schema,* that helped them readily translate the arrangement of pieces into a logical pattern. With the pattern established, they could quickly commit it to memory.

Seminal work in this area (Newell & Simon, 1972) found that mental mod-els are, in fact, what separate experts from novices. When experts encounter a novel problem, they use their mental models (or know-how) to (1) categorize the problem, (2) construct a mental representation of it, (3) search for appropriate problem-solving strategies, (4) retrieve and apply those strategies, (5) evaluate their problem-solving strategies, (6) repeat Steps 1 to 4 if they don't arrive at an immediate solution, and (7) store their experiences for later use. Ultimately, expert mental models reflect a sophisticated integration of declarative knowl-edge (knowing *what kind* of problem they're solving or phenomena they're seeing) and procedural knowledge (knowing *how* to solve the problem or process the information; Nokes et al., 2010).

In contrast, novice learners struggle to solve complex problems because they lack fully formed mental models. For example, when Brand-Gruwel and colleagues (2005) tracked how first-year college students approached research-ing and writing a 400-word essay, they observed that freshmen tended to plunge into the task and spin their wheels poring over superfluous information. Mean-while, doctoral students spent more time sizing up and categorizing the prob-lem and were thus more focused when searching for information. Perhaps most important, graduate students showed a stronger grasp of the writing process itself and continually asked themselves questions like "Is this the information I need? Am I still working toward an answer to my question? How much time do I have left?" The good news is all experts were once novices; your students are novices waiting to become experts. By providing them with structured opportunities to solve problems and observe complex phenomena, you can help them develop and refine their mental models and, thus, build expertise.

Making thinking visible supports development and refinement of mental models

Giving students opportunities to share and explain their thinking can help them develop and refine mental models. Years ago, British researcher Dianne Berry (1983) conducted an experiment that engaged students in solving logical puzzles in three conditions: one group explained their reasoning aloud while solving the puzzles, a second group explained their reasoning *after* solving the puzzles, and a third group solved the puzzles silently. Initially, all three groups showed strong command of puzzles, solving more than 90 percent of them correctly. Yet when tested later to see if they could apply the underlying logic of the puzzles to a similar but new set of puzzles, only the students in the self-explanation group succeeded. Students who hadn't talked through their reasoning while solving the puzzles were unable to transfer the same logic from one set of puzzles to similar, yet new, puzzles. They had learned *how* to solve the puzzles but failed to grasp the logic—or develop a mental model for solving them. For students to truly understand the logic, patterns, or principles of what they're learning, they need to be able to make their thinking visible (to others and to themselves)—and to articulate their own explanation, verbally or in writing, for *why* something works the way it does.

Critical-thinking skills require content knowledge and direct instruction

Critical-thinking skills are regularly heralded as a key competency for students to develop, yet these skills often remain ill-defined. *Critical thinking* is generally defined as the integration of several dispositions and skills, including valuing inquisitiveness and listening to others' points of view, applying logical reasoning to develop and defend arguments, and examining one's own beliefs and changing them in light of new information (Abrami et al., 2015; Bangert-Drowns & Bankert, 1990). Nonetheless, as cognitive scientist Daniel Willingham (2007) noted, critical thinking is not something learned in one subject area and transferred to another. Instead, students must learn and employ, for example, scientific thinking with science knowledge, textual analysis with literature, historical thinking in social studies, quantitative reasoning in mathematics, and so on.

Moreover, according to a meta-analysis of studies of critical-thinking programs (Bangert-Drowns & Bankert, 1990), critical thinking does not develop through osmosis. Merely exposing students to literature, science, history, or geometric proofs does little to develop their critical thinking—instead, they must be *taught* these thinking skills and provided with opportunities to practice. In their study involving over 100 students, Marin and Halpern (2011) compared the performance of students randomly assigned to three groups:

- The first group of students received direct instruction in critical thinking—learning how to develop arguments, parse correlation from causation, identify stereotypes, and predict long-term consequences of decisions.
- The second group engaged in an introduction to psychology workshop with critical thinking embedded into its lessons.
- The control group received regular coursework.

Only the explicit-instruction group demonstrated gains in critical thinking when re-tested on their critical thinking abilities three weeks later.

Cognitively challenging writing tasks support critical thinking

Although writing and critical thinking might seem to be closely linked, research suggests that writing by itself often fails to develop critical thinking, especially for younger students or if writing assignments don't challenge students to engage in high-level thinking (Langer & Applebee, 1987). Quitadamo and Kurtz (2007) randomly assigned college biology students to either write a weekly analytical essay or be quizzed on what they had learned, and found that those in the writing group improved their average critical thinking from the 45th to the 53rd percentile, whereas students in the nonwriting group declined from the 42nd to the 40th percentile. However, in parsing the data, the researchers found that the writing exercises most benefited students who already had strong critical thinking skills, which suggests that writing exercises can *strengthen* but not necessarily *develop* critical thinking. Once again, for students to develop critical thinking skills, these skills need to be directly taught.

Learning through inquiry enhances long-term memory

Reflecting on and responding to high-level questions appears to enhance long-term memory. Pressley and colleagues (1987) found that college students were more likely to recall sentences when they were asked to provide an explanation after reading the sentence (e.g., "Why did the hungry man get in the car?") versus simply reading the sentence (e.g., "A hungry man got into a car to go to restaurant."). From this study and others, cognitive scientists have concluded that "why" questions (sometimes called "elaborative interrogation") may solidify learning by helping to connect new learning with prior knowledge—that is, creating and refining *mental models.*

Consider, for example, what happens in your brain if you're asked to explain exactly why warm air rises. You might think, "Well, I know warm air expands and becomes less dense, just like how air is less dense than water. So, maybe it's like an air bubble rising in a glass of water." In short, pondering a question like this one encourages you to fuse new learning with your existing mental models, which in turn helps your brain "piggyback" new learning onto mental models with pre-existing retrieval hooks. As a result, instead of just having one or two retrieval hooks, you now have several, making it easier for your brain to retrieve what you've learned later.

As it turns out, many early studies pointed to the benefits of engaging students of varied ages and ability levels in inquiry-based learning to support comprehension across multiple content areas (Chi et al., 1994; Scruggs et al., 1994; Schworm & Renkl, 2006; Smith et al., 2010; Wong et al., 2002; Wood & Hewitt, 1993). Nonetheless, research makes clear that inquiry-based learning is most effective when it extends, but does not replace, direct instruction of key ideas and concepts (Woloshyn et al., 1992).

Inquiry and problem solving are most effective when structured and guided

Through a series of studies in the 1980s, Australian researcher John Sweller (1988) concluded that simply throwing students into the deep end of attempting to solve complex problems (e.g., "A car that starts from rest and accelerates uniformly at 2 meters per second squared in a straight line has an average velocity of 17 meters per second. How far has it traveled?") without guidance or scaffolding does little to help students develop problem-solving skills. Novice students must toggle back and forth between figuring out how to solve a problem and actually solving it. If they do arrive (laboriously) at the correct answer, they are unlikely to have developed mental models for solving similar problems in the future.

Along these lines, a meta-analysis of 164 studies (Alfieri et al., 2011) compared the effects of explicit direct instruction versus minimally guided discovery learning (e.g., engaging students in conducting experiments, research, or problem solving with little teacher guidance), and found that students learned significantly more with direct instruction than unassisted discovery learning. Notably, minimally guided learning was particularly ineffective for lower-performing and younger students. Novice learners are prone to learning new skills incorrectly and developing misconceptions (Kirschner et al., 2006). Moreover, they are apt to grow frustrated with discovery learning because of the excessive cognitive load required to switch back and forth between attempting to figure out how to solve a problem and actually solving it (van Merriënboer & Sweller, 2005).

The point here isn't that direct instruction is good and discovery learning is bad. To the contrary, it's that the two strategies work best together (hence, you'll find both in this book). In their meta-analysis of discovery learning, Alfieri and colleagues (2011) found that the best approach—even better than direct instruction—was "guided discovery." Providing students with learning objectives, direct instruction, worked-out examples, and feedback during the process of discovery ensures they develop understandings and proper skills. In the rest of this chapter, we'll explore three evidence-based teaching strategies that strike this balance between student-directed and teacher-supported learning in order to help students extend and apply their learning.

Strategy 12: Cognitive Writing

Cognitive writing engages students in extended writing assignments and supports their comprehension through high-level processing of new learning.

Most of us don't know what we think until we see what we've written. That's because the act of arranging our thoughts into sentences often helps us to arrange them in our minds. So, it's not surprising that several studies in our sample point out the benefits of engaging students in cognitively challenging writing assignments to help them process their learning. Such assignments require students to explain processes and phenomena, analyze and evaluate evidence, develop original ideas, and defend their arguments with evidence. In short, writing should not be confined to language arts classes; it's a powerful tool for deep learning across multiple subject areas. Writing engages students in thinking about what they are learning, sharpens their conceptual understandings, and helps students draw personal connections to their learning. Moreover, cognitive writing isn't simply a matter of putting words onto paper, but rather involves shaping ideas and solidifying enduring understandings in students' minds. We found seven empirical studies of interventions that demonstrated significant effects (improvement index = 14 to 49) for engaging a wide array of students, including ethnically diverse, multilingual, and low-income students in cognitive writing exercises in multiple subject areas (see the Appendix).

Guiding principles for cognitive writing

Cognitive writing structures opportunities for students to think about learning.

Across several studies, writing interventions with positive effects for students were explicitly designed to encourage student thinking through writing. For example, Collins and colleagues (2017) found significant effects for a multiyear writing intervention for racially diverse, low-income elementary students that used "thinksheets," five- to seven-page guides designed to help students extract ideas from text (e.g., "Why do you think it's a good idea for the Iditarod racers to start two minutes apart?"). The intervention also included the use of graphic organizers to arrange ideas (e.g., "Select some evidence and conclusions and put them in the T-chart"). Students responded to prompts designed to encourage cognitive processing of learning (e.g., connecting ideas, comparing and contrasting concepts, developing and defending arguments). After two years, students in the treatment group demonstrated significantly greater gains in reading comprehension (improvement index = 19) than those in the control group, who read the same texts without the benefit of extended writing.

Cognitive writing exercises provide direct instruction in critical-thinking strategies.

Rather than assuming critical-thinking skills develop automatically through writing, effective cognitive writing interventions provide direct instruction in thinking strategies. For example, a series of related experiments in classrooms with racially diverse, low-income, multilingual students (Kim et al., 2011; Olson et al., 2012, 2017) demonstrated significant positive effects (improvement index = 14 to 25). Students were taught a "toolkit" of thinking strategies essential for reading and writing, including setting goals, tapping into prior knowledge, making predictions, identifying main ideas, visualizing, reading text closely, thinking aloud while reading, revising one's own thinking, and self-assessing progress. In keeping with research that shows critical-thinking skills do not develop through osmosis, such interventions show that writing exercises can develop students' thinking skills when they not only challenge students to think deeply about their learning but also provide direct instruction of essential thinking skills.

Cognitive writing exercises should help students extend and apply prior learning.

The effective cognitive writing interventions in all seven studies in our sample were explicitly designed to help students extend and apply learning. For example, Dombek and colleagues (2017) found positive effects for an instructional program that enhanced the science and social studies knowledge of elementary students in racially diverse schools serving low-income neighborhoods by engaging them in the following sequence of learning:

- One day of concept lessons (cueing cognitive interest by connecting learning to students' lives)
- Three to four days of clarifying lessons (e.g., reading about science and social studies)
- Three to four days of research lessons (e.g., conducting science experiments or using primary sources such as photographs, journals, and letters to learn about social studies)
- Three to four days of application lessons (e.g., making connections through challenging learning tasks, including extended writing assignments).

Compared with students in a control group that engaged in more traditional classroom instruction—namely a one- to two-hour "literacy block" focused on literacy instruction alone—students in the treatment group demonstrated significant gains in their knowledge of social studies (improvement index = 49) and science (improvement index = 48). These findings strongly suggest that well-constructed, cognitively challenging writing exercises are a powerful way to help diverse learners build conceptual understanding of prior learning while building their literacy skills.

Classroom tips for cognitive writing

Research has demonstrated the power of helping students extend and apply their learning through writing exercises that challenge them to think deeply about it (comparing, contrasting, evaluating, analyzing, synthesizing), along with direct instruction in the mental tools and strategies needed for deeper thinking and effective writing. Here are some tips for helping students extend and apply their learning through cognitive writing.

Start with what you want students to think about.

As we've previously noted, students only learn what they think about (Willingham, 2003). The key to cognitive writing is ensuring that assignments frame opportunities for students to think about what they are learning. So, as you design writing exercises for students, start with what you want them to think about—the enduring understandings, core concepts, and big ideas. Then, provide writing prompts that engage them in high-level thinking (comparison, analysis, evaluation, synthesis; see Figure 6.1 for some examples).

FIGURE 6.1 SAMPLE WRITING PROMPTS TO ENGAGE STUDENTS IN HIGH-LEVEL THINKING

HIGH-LEVEL THINKING	PROMPT
Comparison	What parallels exist between the Pax Romana and the Pax Americana?
	What are Walter's and Mama's motivations in *A Raisin in the Sun*? How are their motivations different? Alike?
	We read three different versions of what you might know as *Little Red Riding Hood*. How were the characters in each the same and different? How did their actions give you a clue about the setting of the story?
Analysis	How does the author build tension in *The Most Dangerous Game*?
	What genetic adaptations make sharks "nature's perfect predators"?
	You've learned three different ways to solve multiplication problems. Which strategy will you use most often and why? When would you select one of the other two strategies?
Evaluation	Does the film *Citizen Kane* deserve its reputation as one of the greatest of all time?
	Do political parties help or hinder democracy?
	Which of the proposed school garden locations will result in the best growing conditions?
Synthesis	Based on our previous readings, should nonnative species be banned from importation?
	Based on our previous readings, should young people be given access to social media?
	Based on our readings in this unit, which inventions have changed our lives the most?

Directly teach and model thinking skills.

Writing by itself does little to help students learn or develop thinking skills. At best, writing exercises provide students with opportunities to *practice*—but not develop—critical thinking skills. To help students truly engage in cognitive writing, teach them the thinking skills that are essential for the task. As with any skill, provide students with direct instruction and modeling of each of these skills, showing them how effective writers (and thinkers) employ them. Figure 6.2 lists of some of these key skills along with a description of how each is used.

FIGURE 6.2   THINKING SKILLS USED IN COGNITIVE WRITING

THINKING SKILL	HOW IT'S DEPLOYED
Understanding the task	Before plunging into writing, effective writers carefully read the prompt and ask clarifying questions to ensure they understand the task.
Setting goals	Strong writers set mastery goals for their writing (e.g., I want to use relevant data to persuade my readers that school should start later in the morning).
Reflecting on prior knowledge	While gathering evidence, effective writers reflect on their prior knowledge and how what they are learning supports, modifies, or conflicts with what they already know.
Extracting and expressing key ideas	Effective writers extract key ideas from a source and restate them in their own words (e.g., How would you explain this concept to a friend or family member?).
Developing and revisiting a main idea	Strong writers develop a key idea, thesis statement, or central argument and periodically revisit their idea, revising it as needed.
Showing, not telling	Effective writers support their arguments with concrete examples and details that "show" readers what they're telling them.
Considering and responding to counter-arguments	After completing an initial draft, strong writers reread their writing, anticipating how others might respond to their arguments, and offer new arguments or evidence to strengthen their arguments.
Self-monitoring and self-assessing progress	Strong writers continually ask themselves, "Am I on track? Is this evidence important? Am I accomplishing my goal?"
Revising one's own thinking	Strong writers are flexible thinkers, able to revisit and clarify their ideas as they encounter new evidence or develop better ideas.

Develop tools and guides to structure cognitive writing.

In addition to teaching thinking skills directly, it's helpful to provide students with visual tools and guides to help them to think about their learning, arrange their thoughts, and put them on paper. The example in Figure 6.3 (see p. 116) reflects the "thinksheets" Collins and colleagues (2017) demonstrated to be highly effective in supporting the success of diverse learners.

Develop and provide rubrics for all cognitive writing assignments.

Rubrics are powerful classroom tools—not because they help teachers evaluate student work more objectively but because they make learning expectations

FIGURE 6.3   GUIDED INVESTIGATIONS BASED ON THE SIX-PHASE
LEARNING MODEL

Key Thinking Strategy: _____
(e.g., compare, analyze, synthesize)

Directions
As you read this text, pay close attention to ___.

Guiding Questions
Why do you think ___ ? Why should __ occur?

Arrange Your Thinking and Writing
List key arguments and evidence
List key ideas and examples

clear for students. For all major writing tasks, provide students with a rubric to make learning expectations clear across multiple dimensions: developing and sharing original ideas, supporting arguments with evidence and examples, writing clearly, and editing to avoid spelling mistakes and grammatical errors. Figure 6.4 offers an example of a writing rubric designed to promote a growth mindset by avoiding labels like "inadequate" or "poor" and opting instead for growth-oriented terms like "developing" and "emerging."

Provide students with opportunities to share and revise their writing.
Several effective cognitive writing interventions have incorporated peer-assisted consolidation—often in the form of writer's workshops. As it turns out, when students realize their peers (not just their teachers) will read their writing, they often become more motivated to invest time and effort into their writing. This helps them develop more compelling ideas, defend them, and write more clearly. Giving students opportunities to share their writing with peers, see others' writing, and receive feedback on their own writing can support deeper thinking about learning as well as improved writing—especially if you provide a rubric to support peer feedback, self-reflection, revisions, and editing.

FIGURE 6.4   A WRITING RUBRIC DESIGNED TO PROMOTE A GROWTH MINDSET

CRITERIA	EMERGING	DEVELOPING	MEETS EXPECTATIONS	EXEMPLARY
Ideas and supporting details	Central idea is missing or vague and few supporting details provided	Central idea is stated but inadequately supported (i.e., more telling than showing)	Central idea is stated and supported with details (i.e., showing not telling)	Central idea reflects original thinking and is well supported with details
Organization and transitions	Organizational structure is difficult to follow; few transition words used	Organizational structure is mostly evident and logical, but use of transition words to guide readers is inconsistent	Organizational structure is consistently evident and logical; transition words consistently guide readers	Writing is clearly organized and logical, with a variety of strong transition words used to guide readers
Voice and word choice	Few strong verbs and little use of precise language or key vocabulary	Inconsistent use of strong verbs and precise language or vocabulary	Consistently uses strong verbs and precise language or vocabulary	Makes many good language choices to develop a strong, engaging voice
Conventions and spelling	Many grammatical or proofreading errors are evident, and they interfere with understanding	Some distracting grammatical or proofreading errors are evident, and they may interfere with understanding	Final draft reflects some grammatical or proofreading errors, but they do not interfere with understanding	Final draft reflects very few grammatical or proofreading errors

Strategy 13: Guided Investigations

Guided investigations engage students in experiments, inquiry-based learning, and research projects that require high levels of cognitive engagement.

Conventional forms of classroom learning fail to stick for many students; they typically forget 90 percent of it within 30 days (Medina, 2008). This is because students have too few opportunities to not only repeat but also *retrieve* their learning in multiple ways and contexts. Guided investigations engage students in exploring compelling questions, observing real-world phenomena, analyzing data and evidence, and reporting their discoveries. Such opportunities support long-term memory in two powerful ways. First, they tap into students' natural curiosity to make learning more joyful and memorable for them. They also provide students with opportunities to use repetition and retrieval to encode their learning more richly.

The two previous editions of *Classroom Instruction That Works* identified a category of strategies called "generating and testing hypotheses," which included several teaching strategies such as systems analysis, problem solving, experimental inquiry, and investigation. Over the past decade, many new empirical studies have extended and further clarified this category of effective teaching practices, leading us to highlight two related yet separate approaches to project-based learning: guided investigations and structured problem solving. Guided investigations engage students in examining driving questions and investigating intriguing phenomena, primarily in natural and social sciences and typically with the following sequence of learning activities:

1. Build students' background knowledge with high-interest texts.
2. Design experiments and investigations to test hypotheses and assumptions.
3. Collect data and gather evidence through close observation and reading.
4. Use evidence to support findings and conclusions.

Our review of research yielded eight empirical studies with significant positive effect sizes (improvement index = 10 to 49) for using guided investigations to support student learning in science, social studies, and in some cases, reading (see the Appendix). These positive effects were found for a variety of student groups, including students in poverty, emergent bilingual students, and students with learning disabilities.

Guiding principles for guided investigations

The following principles for guided investigations emerge from these studies.

Thinking deeply about learning helps students to encode new learning in long-term memory.

As with cognitive writing, the main purpose of guided investigations isn't simply to have students *do something* with their learning but rather to give them opportunities to *think deeply about* their learning while doing something with it. This encodes new learning more richly and deeply in their long-term memories. Often, one of the best ways to get students to think about their learning is to encourage them to examine and re-examine their preconceived notions (i.e., mental models) about scientific phenomena, social issues, and historical events. For example, an inquiry-based middle school science curriculum introduced culturally and racially diverse middle school students to concepts and phenomena that contradicted their preconceived mental models (Lynch et al., 2007). Through structured learning activities, students investigated conflicting ideas, reflected on their thinking and how it might be changing, discussed their ideas and observations with others, and engaged in "think and write" exercises that guided them in interpreting data and sharing their evolving thinking. Students experienced significant gains in science learning (improvement index = 10).

Student self-direction should be balanced with teacher-guided learning.

Decades of research has shown that minimally guided learning has limited benefits for students (Alfieri et al., 2011) and may be particularly harmful for low-achieving students (Kirschner et al., 2006). The key is to balance student self-direction with teacher direction. The Chemistry That Applies curriculum (Lynch et al., 2007) reflected this balance between student self-direction and teacher direction by engaging students in independent learning activities. Their inquiry was structured by teacher-provided questions that encouraged them to reflect on prior knowledge, consider key questions (e.g., "How do your predictions compare to the actual changes in the weights of substances?"), design a plan to test predictions and collect data, and organize and interpret data.

Lorch and colleagues (2010) tested whether lectures or hand-on experiments are more effective. Specifically, they compared the effects of three different approaches to science instruction for 4th grade students: (1) classroom lectures, (2) hands-on experiments, or (3) a combination of both. As it turns out, students in the combined lecture and experiments group outperformed those in instruction-only group (improvement index = 12) as well as those in the experiment-only group (improvement index = 27). Notably, although students from higher-performing schools demonstrated gains in all three conditions, those in the experimentation-only condition from high-poverty, low-performing schools showed no learning gains whatsoever. This reinforces earlier research findings that minimally guided instruction may be particularly detrimental for lower-achieving students. Given competing views of direct instruction versus discovery learning, educators might reasonably wonder, "Should I use direct instruction or discovery learning?" Research suggests the answer is yes—that is, both are effective, especially when used together. A well-delivered and interactive lecture or demonstration of skills can be highly effective for introducing students to new ideas and skills, helping them focus on new learning. Guided investigations, meanwhile, can help students extend and apply what they've learned so that they embed it more deeply in their long-term memories.

Hands-on and real-world learning experiences deepen learning.

Guthrie and colleagues (2006) conducted a "natural experiment" that compared the outcomes of 98 elementary students learning the same science content, reading the same texts, and receiving the same amount of science instruction—with one key difference. In two classrooms, teachers stimulated high levels of student interest by engaging them in hands-on learning activities and observations, posing more science questions, and encouraging students to generate and test more hypotheses (Guthrie et al., 2006). Although students did not differ in terms of prior achievement or demographics (all were in high-poverty schools), after just 12 weeks, those in high-stimulation classrooms demonstrated significantly higher reading comprehension than those in low-stimulation classrooms (improvement index = 26).

Guided investigations, especially those that engage students in hands-on learning activities related to texts and classroom-based learning, also have positive effects on student motivation and achievement. Friedman and colleagues (2017) found that the Playground Physics program enhanced science learning of middle schoolers (improvement index = 15). This program provided students with a series of structured lessons and a software application to record videos of each other engaging in playground activities, which students viewed through "lenses" designed to illustrate scientific principles of motion. Other effective interventions have included engaging students in dissecting owl pellets to better understand ecology (improvement index = 26; Guthrie et al., 2004) and adjusting the slope and surface of ramps to comprehend the physics of motion (improvement index = 27; Lorch et al., 2010). Notably, in all cases, hands-on activities were not simply "fun" diversions from learning but explicitly designed to help students extend and apply their learning.

Cognitive writing exercises can help ensure guided investigations support deep learning.

Guided investigations may include cognitive writing exercises designed to help students consolidate and deepen their learning. Here are some examples: August and colleagues (2009) studied a program called Quality English and Science Teaching (QuEST), which integrated several evidence-based teaching strategies, including cognitive interest cues, direct instruction of vocabulary, peer-assisted consolidation of learning, hands-on experiments, *and* writing assignments. Dombek and colleagues (2017) found that a structured learning sequence—three to four days of science experiments or using primary sources in social studies, followed by three to four days of cognitive writing exercises— increased students' science and social studies knowledge. Similarly, a guided-inquiry curriculum supported gains in science learning for diverse middle school students, including many with learning disabilities (Lynch et al., 2007). The curriculum paired science experiments with "think and write" exercises designed to help students interpret data and the results of their experiments. And, finally, a literacy-integrated science unit paired hands-on exploration activities with frequent reading and writing exercises and demonstrated positive effects in improving the science knowledge of diverse groups of students from low-socioeconomic status backgrounds (Tong et al., 2014).

Classroom tips for guided investigations

Hands-on learning experiences let students explore, think deeply about, and consolidate enduring understandings. Here are some tips to help you engage your students to extend and apply their learning with guided investigations.

Start with what students should think about—and what they need to see to believe and comprehend.

As with cognitive writing, it's important to anchor guided investigations in the enduring understandings you want your students to develop. What discoveries should they make? What "aha" moments should they have? What new insights should they develop? As the saying goes, seeing is believing. Consider which discoveries and insights students may need to see (via investigations or hands-on experiments) to believe or comprehend. For example, students might not actually believe that heavier objects fall at the same rate as lighter objects until they see it happen with their own eyes. Likewise, they might not appreciate the differences sunlight, soil, and water have on plant growth until they observe these for themselves.

Identify what knowledge and skills to teach directly and what students should discover.

As we've noted, minimally guided discovery learning is rarely effective. However, *guided* discovery, which integrates teacher direction with student discovery, is incredibly powerful. As you design a guided investigation, consider the following questions:

- What knowledge or skills (e.g., observation, prediction, classification, analysis) do students need to conduct the investigation?
- Which key concepts and vocabulary terms (e.g., titration, catalyst, reaction) do they need to understand to conduct the investigation or interpret findings?
- Do you want your students to discover concepts first and hear them explained afterward?

Ensure students return to thinking about key concepts, big ideas, and enduring understandings.

It's easy for students (and teachers) to become so engrossed in the process of investigation that they lose sight of its purpose—namely, to develop deep understandings of natural phenomena, social issues, or historical events. In short, investigations can become more about *doing* than *thinking*. Given that students only learn what they think about, be sure to anchor investigations in opportunities for students to think about and reflect on what they've learned through class discussions and writing exercises that ultimately connect back to learning goals.

Use the learning model to design your investigation.

As it turns out, a well-designed guided investigation should reflect all six phases of learning. Figure 6.5 illustrates how a guided investigation can be set up to incorporate all six phases of learning.

FIGURE 6.5   GUIDED INVESTIGATIONS BASED ON THE SIX-PHASE LEARNING MODEL

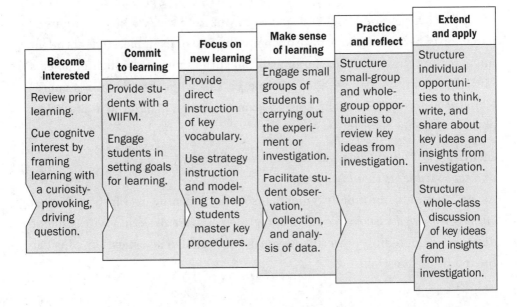

Become interested	Commit to learning	Focus on new learning	Make sense of learning	Practice and reflect	Extend and apply
Review prior learning. Cue cognitve interest by framing learning with a curiosity-provoking, driving question.	Provide students with a WIIFM. Engage students in setting goals for learning.	Provide direct instruction of key vocabulary. Use strategy instruction and modeling to help students master key procedures.	Engage small groups of students in carrying out the experiment or investigation. Facilitate student observation, collection, and analysis of data.	Structure small-group and whole-group opportunities to review key ideas from investigation.	Structure individual opportunities to think, write, and share about key ideas and insights from investigation. Structure whole-class discussion of key ideas and insights from investigation.

Strategy 14: Structured Problem Solving

Structured problem solving develops mental schema by teaching step-by-step processes for understanding and applying knowledge and skills to solve complex, real-life problems.

Research points to another strategy with proven effects in helping students extend and apply learning—particularly with math and quantitative reasoning skills: *structured problem solving*. Unlike more open-ended cognitive writing or guided investigations, structured problem solving typically engages students in searching for an answer to a complex problem or set of problems. Nonetheless, the journey to the answer is as important as the answer itself. In many cases, a key element of structured problem solving is the explicit focus on helping students develop mental schema—that is, the ability to recognize the kind of problem they are solving even as the particulars of the problems change. Many studies that support this strategy, in fact, refer to it as "schema-based" or "schema-broadening" instruction.

Twelve scientific studies in our sample reported significant positive effects (improvement index = 16–48) for structured problem solving with a variety of student groups, including racially diverse students, students in poverty, emergent bilingual students, and students with learning disabilities (see the Appendix). Although most of these interventions focused on mathematics learning, one study (Vaughn et al., 2017) reported positive effects for a form of structured problem solving in social studies.

Guiding principles for structured problem solving

The following guiding principles for structured problem solving emerge from these studies.

Anchoring learning in real-life problems enhances student motivation and problem-solving skills.

We're all familiar with word problems that no one needs to solve in the real world, such as the clichéd "One train leaves St. Louis at 8:00 a.m. and another leaves Chicago at 9:00 a.m. When do they meet?" (*Answer:* Who cares?). Structured problem solving does not simply engage students in solving meaningless word problems. Instead, it challenges students to solve interesting problems that are anchored to real-world challenges and hands-on learning activities relevant to them. Bottge and colleagues (2002, 2014, 2015) demonstrated positive effects for "enhanced anchored instruction," cueing students' interest with videos of students attempting to solve complex, real-world problems (e.g., calculating the costs and sales tax of lumber and materials needed to build a skateboard ramp, designing ramps with the right height and slope to get model cars to perform loops and other tricks). The problem-solving activities themselves culminated in hands-on learning—students building ramps to test their calculations. Compared to engaging students in traditional classroom instruction, providing enhanced anchored instruction had significant benefits for previously low-achieving students (improvement index = 26 to 38).

Students need direct instruction in problem-solving schemas.

Multiple studies point to the power of providing students with direct instruction in learning to identify the type of problem they are solving, retrieve prior learning to solve problems, and reflect on strategies while using them. For example, Fuchs and colleagues (2004) examined the effects of schema-based transfer instruction (SBTI) for 300-plus 3rd grade students engaged in solving complex, real-world math problems. Students in the first treatment condition received explicit instruction in identifying the type of problems they were solving and what strategies were needed to solve them. Students in a second treatment condition received an expanded version of SBTI that exposed them to even more complex real-world problems with more superficial details in problem cover stories to help students develop the ability to recognize the underlying schema of the problems. After 16 weeks, students in the expanded SBTI group significantly outperformed the SBTI group (improvement index = 36), which in turn outperformed a control group receiving business-as-usual instruction (improvement index = 30). Students clearly benefit from direct instruction in how to parse surface details in problems to identify underlying similarities across problem types; this in turn helps them develop and broaden mental schema for solving problems. Simple mnemonics can help students remember problem-solving processes, such as RUN (Read the problem, Underline key words, Name the problem type; Fuchs et al., 2021) and FOPS (Find the problem, Organize information using a diagram, Plan to solve the problem, Solve the problem; Jitendra et al., 2011, 2013).

Think-alouds and student self-explanations can enhance structured problem solving.

Mental models are a powerful form of self-talk, serving as a voice in students' heads that guides them through problem solving (e.g., "What kind of problem is this?" "Have I solved something like it before?" "What strategies do I need to use?"). Many students, especially those who initially struggle to solve complex problems, have yet to fully develop this voice in their heads. Think-alouds and self-explanations appear to be effective in helping them develop this voice. Jitendra and colleagues (2009), for example, demonstrated positive effects of encouraging students to use think-alouds while employing the FOPS strategy (e.g., "Did I read and retell the problem to understand what is given and what must be solved?"). A control group received regular, textbook-based instruction on ratios and proportions that included worked-out examples to scaffold problem solving. Students in the think-aloud treatment group demonstrated significantly better performance on both immediate and delayed post-tests of problem-solving abilities (improvement index = 17 and 21, respectively).

Direct instruction of vocabulary enhances the effects of structured problem solving.

Given that words are the pegs upon which we hang ideas, it's not surprising that studies find positive effects for incorporating vocabulary instruction into structured problem solving. Fuchs and colleagues (2021), for example, found that embedding direct instruction of academic vocabulary (e.g., "more," "fewer than," "cost," "because") into schema-based instruction (SBI) yielded significant gains for students versus SBI alone (improvement index = 36) and even greater gains over business-as-usual instruction (improvement index = 46). Similarly, Vaughn and colleagues (2017) assessed the benefits of teaching 8th grade students (including a large number of emergent bilingual students) essential vocabulary terms prior to engaging them in small-group problem-solving activities (e.g., responding to such questions as "How did the colonial regions develop differently?" or "What might have happened to prevent the Revolutionary War?"). These students demonstrated greater gains over a business-as-usual control group on measures of content knowledge (improvement index = 16) and reading comprehension (improvement index = 8).

Helping students recognize problem structures can close learning gaps.

Structured problem solving appears to be particularly beneficial for students with prior low levels of achievement. A primary cause of math learning difficulties—especially as students engage in complex problem solving—is students' inability to recognize problem types, filter relevant from irrelevant information, and draw upon their prior learning to solve problems. Xin and colleagues (2005) compared the effects of two problem-solving instructional approaches—SBI and general strategy instruction—on the word problem-solving abilities of middle school students with learning disabilities or low prior math achievement. All students were taught a four-step process for solving word problems: (1) read to understand, (2) develop a plan, (3) solve, and (4) look back. Those in the treatment group, though, also received explicit instruction in identifying problem types and using diagrams to represent problems. The treatment group significantly outperformed the control group on immediate and delayed post-tests as well as a transfer test (improvement index = 45, 49, and 50, respectively). These results suggest that structured problem solving can be particularly beneficial for students with prior low achievement when they are given both direct instruction in recognizing problem types and visual aids to guide them through the problem-solving process.

Effective structured problem-solving assignments integrate other proven instructional strategies.

Collectively, these studies reveal that structured problem solving is not a single strategy but actually the integration of many proven strategies, including the following:

- **Cognitive interest cues**—using videos and real-world problems to enhance student interest and motivation in solving complex problems (Bottge et al., 2002, 2014, 2015; Fuchs et al., 2004)
- **Student goal setting**—helping students develop self-regulated learning strategies for solving complex problems, including using goal setting and positive self-talk to stay on task (Fuchs, Fuchs, et al., 2008)
- **Visualizations and concrete examples**—providing students with multiple representations of math problems (Bottge et al., 2014, 2015; Fuchs, Fuchs, et al., 2008) and creating visual representations of problems prior to solving them (Jitendra et al., 2011, 2013)
- **Direct instruction and modeling**—providing explicit direct instruction to help students develop schema for solving complex problems (Bottge et al., 2002, 2015; Fuchs et al., 2004, 2021; Fuchs, Schumacher, et al., 2013; Jitendra et al., 2011, 2013; Xin et al., 2005)
- **Academic vocabulary instruction**—building student knowledge of key academic and subject-specific vocabulary terms prior to engaging in complex problem solving (Fuchs et al., 2021; Vaughn et al., 2017)

- **Peer-assisted consolidation of learning**—engaging small groups of students in solving complex problems (Bottge et al., 2015; Vaughn et al., 2017)
- **High-level questions and student self-explanations**—providing high-level questions and encouraging students to think aloud to monitor their problem solving (Jitendra et al., 2009, 2013)

In short, structured problem solving is not a stand-alone strategy but an umbrella approach that integrates teaching strategies from the previous five phases of learning (becoming interested, committing to learning, focusing on new learning, making sense of learning, and practicing and reflecting). It's about helping students extend and apply their learning *after* they have fully engaged in the first five phases.

Classroom tips for structured problem solving

Collectively, these studies demonstrate the power of engaging students in solving complex, real-world problems while providing structure and guidance to help them develop mental models needed to recognize the underlying structure or problems and retrieve the appropriate problem-solving strategies. Here are some tips to help you translate these principles into learning opportunities that build your students' mental models and problem-solving skills.

Anchor learning in complex and relatable problems.

Challenging puzzles are a powerful driver of curiosity and intrinsic motivation (Loewenstein, 1994); people will happily subject themselves to the brow-furrowing frustration of daily crosswords, jigsaw puzzles, and escape rooms. Students are no different. Few hop out of bed in the morning worrying about when a train from St. Louis will arrive in Chicago, but if they can encounter extension and application activities they see as challenging problems that relate to their own interests and lives, they are more likely to be engaged and motivated to learn. The key here is finding a strong, culturally relevant anchor for learning—a realistic scenario (often framed as a story or adventure featuring main characters confronting a problem) with multiple subproblems that require students to analyze data in order to develop a plausible solution for the characters in the story (Bottge, 2001). Figure 6.6 (see p. 128) lists some possible topic areas and ways to anchor problems in students' interests.

FIGURE 6.6   EXAMPLES OF STRUCTURED PROBLEMS ANCHORED
IN MEANINGFUL CHALLENGES

TOPIC AREA	EXAMPLES
Building and construction problems	Calculating the materials and costs for building skateboard ramps, sets for school plays, backyard projects, robotics projects
Environmental challenges	Calculating energy and cost savings of conservation, waste reduction, or recycling; measuring the carbon output of various forms of school transportation
Financial puzzles	Calculating total net earnings of various professions; creating a budget and calculating accrued savings; determining best value of cell phone plans
Health challenges	Calculating calories burned during various forms of exercise; correlating links between mental well-being and social media usage or sleep habits
Sports challenges	Calculating speed and arc of a 3-point basketball shot, ideal pitching distance to increase batter reaction time, whether to punt or go for first down in football

Provide your students with a process—and memory aid— for tackling complex problems.

Without proper scaffolding, problem-based learning can leave students confused or with underdeveloped mental models and little ability to solve similar yet novel problems. Be sure to teach your students a process for tackling complex problems, such as the following:

1. **Grasp the problem**—What's important? What's extraneous? What kind of problem is this?

2. **Plan a course of action**—What strategy(ies) should I use? How would I list or draw them?

3. **Work the problem**—What steps are required? Am I doing them correctly?

4. **Review the solution**—Does it make sense? If not, what should I do differently? If so, what's important to remember the next time I encounter a similar problem?

In addition to teaching students the problem-solving process, you may want to provide a mnemonic or simple acronym to remember it, such as RUN (Fuchs et al., 2021), FOPS (Jitendra et al., 2013), or one that you come up with on your own or with your students.

Help students recognize and categorize problem types.

A key element for building schema is helping students recognize problem types and access strategies for solving them, and teaching both practices directly to students. Figure 6.7 offers a starter list of problem categories, their definitions, and strategies for solving them.

FIGURE 6.7   PROBLEM TYPES AND SOLUTION STRATEGIES

PROBLEM TYPE	DEFINITION	COMMON SOLUTION STRATEGIES
Grouping problems	Grouping problems use addition or multiplication to combine two smaller parts or groups into a larger one. Alternatively, they may start with the total amount and use subtraction or division to calculate the subgroups.	Add numbers together to calculate the sum of the parts (e.g., across 6th, 7th, and 8th grade, our school has 607 students). Subtract a lesser number from a greater one to determine the size of a smaller group or part (e.g., we added 204 new 6th graders this year).
Change problems	Change problems have a beginning, middle, and ending. One quantity changes to another through some form of direct action (e.g., a savings account accrues interest).	Add, multiply, subtract the change amount to/by/from the beginning quantity to create the ending quantity (e.g., you now have $107 in savings). Subtract the ending quantity from the beginning quantity to determine change (e.g., your savings grew 3 percent this month).
Compare problems	Compare problems focus on static differences between unrelated sets (e.g., Ty is 4 inches taller than Tyra, who is 3 inches taller than Tyrell).	Add or subtract comparative quantities of one set to calculate properties of another set (e.g., Ty is 5'11", Tyra is 5'7", Tyrell is 5'4"). Divide the quantity of the greater set by the quantity of the lesser set to calculate percentage differences (e.g., Tyra is 94% as tall as Ty).

Help students use graphic organizers and drawings to visualize problems.

In addition to memory aids, graphic organizers help students visualize problems, organize key information, and make abstract concepts more concrete—thereby reducing the cognitive demand of problem solving (Jitendra et al., 2011, 2013). The example in Figure 6.8 (see p. 130) illustrates how graphic organizers can support structured problem solving.

FIGURE 6.8   AN EXAMPLE OF GRAPHIC ORGANIZER USE IN STRUCTURED PROBLEM SOLVING

Mr. Smith needs the stage crew of the school musical to build a plywood backdrop that is 8 feet high and 64 feet wide. Currently, there are seven 8- x 4-foot plywood panels in the storage room. How many additional panels are needed to build the backdrop? And how much will it cost to buy these panels if each panel costs $19.45?

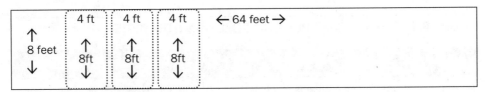

1. The first step is a *grouping* problem: we must calculate how many sheets are required all together. If each panel is 4 feet wide, how many will cover 64 feet? *Number sentence: 64 ÷ 4 = x.* It may help to draw a picture like this:

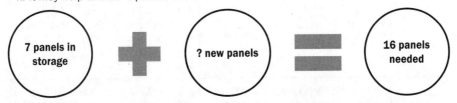

2. OK, so we know we need 16 panels to cover the space. Now we must calculate how many additional sheets are needed, which is a *change* problem. We start with one quantity and, through action, end with another, like this:

3. Like many **change** problems, we can subtract a lesser number from a greater number to arrive at an answer. *Number sentence: 16 – 7 = x*

4. Now we must calculate the cost of 9 additional panels if each one costs $19.45. We might picture it like this:

5. We could add these numbers together, but is there a simpler way? *Number sentence: 9 x $19.45 = x*

Now we know the answer: $175.05. Looks like the Drama Club will need to sell a lot of tickets to cover these costs!

Teach students the metacognitive skills and positive self-talk needed to solve complex problems.

A key purpose of structured problem solving is to challenge students cognitively—to engage them in "productive struggle" that stretches their thinking while developing the persistence required to tackle complex problems. Many effective interventions have supported student self-regulation and positive self-talk (Fuchs, Fuchs, et al., 2008; Jitendra et al., 2009; Xin et al., 2005) by providing direct instruction in self-regulation and thinking skills, setting and tracking progress toward goals, listening carefully, following directions, and guiding oneself back to the task at hand. Here are a few key phrases and questions students can use to help themselves persist through structured problem solving:

- Do I understand the directions? What's still fuzzy or unclear?
- Can I visualize what's happening with this problem?
- What's my goal? Am I getting closer to it?
- Am I getting distracted? What can I do to get myself back on task?
- Don't give up! Struggle makes my brain stronger.

Final Thoughts: The Missing Components in Many Classrooms

The three strategies highlighted in this chapter may be the most important in this book because of their proven ability to help students convert new information into deep learning. Yet in many classrooms, they are conspicuously absent, with learning stopping abruptly with summative assessments. And if this final phase of learning is lopped off, students are likely to forget most of what they "mastered." On top of that, they may view the entire process of schooling as a perfunctory exercise of taking tests on content and skills that are hopelessly divorced from real life, meaning, and interest. In a word, schooling will feel like drudgery.

That's not what you signed up for when you entered the teaching profession. You became an educator to instill in students a desire to become learners and gain knowledge and skills they can and will use over a lifetime. The good news is that, with the 14 strategies highlighted in this book, you can do exactly that.

7

Bringing It All Together

When we set out to create another edition of a text as influential as *Classroom Instruction That Works,* we worried it might be a fool's errand, akin to attempting a sequel to film classics like *Citizen Kane* or *Casablanca.* Some readers, we figured, would be disappointed if we did not hew closely to the original. Others, we worried, might be dismayed if the new edition lacked significantly new insights or guidance.

With this edition, we hope we've split the difference by following the spirit of the earlier editions—using best available research to advance the science of teaching—while taking a fresh look at the research itself. This effort included focusing on a new generation of empirical studies viewed through the lens of the science of learning and acknowledging the diversity of learners in our schools. The result, we believe, is something that educators will find to be both fresh *and* grounded in the earlier editions.

Bridging *The New Classroom Instruction That Works* with Earlier Editions

Nonetheless, given the popularity of the previous editions and the fact that thousands of teachers worldwide have used the information in the earlier books as a framework for teaching, we anticipate some readers may wonder how the 14 strategies in this book relate to the 9 categories of instruction in the first and second editions. Figure 7.1 offers a "crosswalk" that illustrates how the new strategies build upon and expand the earlier categories.

FIGURE 7.1   CROSSWALK OF NEW STRATEGIES AND THE ORIGINAL CATEGORIES OF INSTRUCTION

ORIGINAL *CITW* CATEGORY	UPDATED RESEARCH	*NEW CITW* STRATEGIES
Setting objectives and providing feedback	Most studies included in the previous editions do not meet new criteria for experimental research. Related studies in the new research base support student goal setting as well as guided initial application with formative feedback.	• Student goal setting and monitoring • Guided initial application with formative feedback
Reinforcing effort and providing recognition	Studies from previous editions do not meet new criteria for experimental research. Some studies that support student goal setting reflect reinforcing effort.	• Student goal setting and monitoring
Cooperative learning	Most studies included in previous editions do not meet new criteria for experimental research. Studies in the new research base support peer-assisted consolidation of learning (versus using groups to introduce new learning).	• Peer-assisted consolidation of learning
Cues, questions, and advance organizers	Most studies included in previous editions do not meet new criteria for experimental research. Studies in the new research base support cognitive interest cues as well as high-level questions and student explanations.	• Cognitive interest cues • High-level questions and student explanations
Nonlinguistic representations	Studies in previous editions do not meet new criteria for experimental research. Studies in the new research base support visualizations and concrete examples.	• Visualizations and concrete examples
Summarizing and note taking	Most studies included in previous editions do not meet new criteria for experimental research. Prior studies retained in the new research base support strategy instruction and modeling (i.e., direct instruction for summarizing texts) and cognitive writing (i.e., using writing to synthesize learning).	• Strategy instruction and modeling • Cognitive writing
Assigning homework and practice	Studies supporting homework do not meet new criteria for experimental research. Most studies supporting practice did not meet criteria; those retained in the new research base support retrieval practice as well as interleaved and spaced practice.	• Retrieval practice (quizzing to remember) • Spaced, mixed independent practice

continued

FIGURE 7.1　CROSSWALK OF NEW STRATEGIES AND THE ORIGINAL CATEGORIES OF INSTRUCTION *(continued)*

ORIGINAL *CITW* CATEGORY	UPDATED RESEARCH	NEW *CITW* STRATEGIES
Identifying similarities and differences	Studies in previous editions do not meet new criteria for experimental research. Those included in the new research base support cognitive interest cues (using metaphors to link new and prior learning) and schema-based instruction (helping students compare new problems with prior problems).	• Cognitive interest cues • Structured problem solving
Generating and testing hypotheses	Studies included in previous editions do not meet new criteria for experimental research. Studies in the new research base support cognitive writing, guided investigations, and structured problem solving.	• Cognitive writing • Guided investigations • Structured problem solving

Three new effective teaching strategies that were not identified in previous editions of *Classroom Instruction That Works* emerged from new empirical studies:

- Vocabulary instruction
- Strategy instruction and modeling
- Targeted supports (scaffolded practice)

As noted earlier, all three of these strategies have been shown to have powerful effects on student learning and, thus, represent important additions to teachers' repertoires.

With each new empirical study, the science of teaching continues to evolve, offering new and more precise insights. Indeed, we anticipate that, as the science of teaching and learning continues to evolve, in a decade or two we may come to view these new strategies in a different light and be able to offer teachers even more precise guidance. Nonetheless, what we can say definitively is that the best available current research has identified the 14 strategies we've highlighted in this book as having powerful effects on student learning. Thus, students are well served when teachers apply them in their classrooms.

Getting from here to there

Like anyone learning new techniques, no one is apt to master all 14 strategies overnight. Mastering even just one strategy takes time, including multiple cycles of practice, reflection, and revision. The first time you attempt to apply one of these strategies in your classroom, it may feel awkward or fall flat. That's to be expected. With that in mind, we offer the following guidelines to help you and your colleagues translate these strategies into practice in your classrooms and school.

Focus on the strategy that offers the best opportunity for growth for you.

We recognize there's a lot to learn in this book. We do not expect any teacher or school to attempt to apply them all at once (or be successful in doing so). Rather, we suggest you first identify your bright spots—the strategies you have already mastered and can apply consistently in your classroom. Acknowledge your current strengths while recognizing that your energies are best spent targeting your professional learning on your most pressing problem of practice.

You might consider, for example, which of the six phases of learning represent your biggest classroom challenge. As we noted in *Learning That Sticks* (Goodwin et al., 2020), the six-phase learning model can serve as a helpful diagnostic tool for identifying where the process of learning may be breaking down or lagging in your classroom. For example, do you struggle most to engage students in their learning? If so, you might start with cognitive interest cues. Do too many students require Tier 2 targeted supports? You may decide to focus on improving Tier 1 instruction by delivering more consistent and effective strategy instruction and modeling. The point here is that your focus should be *your own*—where tangible improvements in teaching are most likely to yield the biggest gains in student learning.

Don't go it alone.

An unfortunate practice we see persisting in many schools is that of teachers continuing to engage in "private practice"—teaching in isolation behind closed classroom doors with limited interaction with colleagues. As a result, many educators have few opportunities to learn from each other or work together to embed better practices into their classrooms. Yet research has shown (Joyce & Showers, 2002) that very little professional learning translates into classroom practice without peer-to-peer coaching. Teachers need to observe and coach one another—not in a finger-wagging way but as a support system for improving and refining everyone's professional practice. If you're reading this book independently, we congratulate you on your professional curiosity. Nonetheless, we encourage you to share it with a trusted colleague so that you can work together to apply these practices in your classrooms.

Stick with it.

Any behavior change—whether it's eschewing fries in favor of salads or committing to an exercise routine—takes time. Adopting new teaching practices is no different. Each new strategy takes significant time to embed in classroom practices. Moreover, even after you incorporate a new practice into your teaching repertoire, it's easy to slide back into old habits, as Mary Budd Rowe (1986) discovered years ago while helping teachers embed wait time in their teaching practice. Although most teachers could quickly understand and incorporate longer wait time in their teaching, after just a few weeks, many reverted to old habits. To make best practices your own, you must stick with them for weeks, months, and even years. And it's much easier to stick with better practices when you (1) stay focused and (2) work with others to implement these practices.

Adopt and adapt.

Despite our best efforts to illustrate what these practices look like across different subject areas, grade levels, and student groups, you will need to contextualize them and adapt them for your own students. What's most important here isn't fidelity to a particular program but, rather, fidelity to *guiding principles*—that is, the deeper underlying purpose of a strategy or *why* it supports student learning. This is why we've offered not only tips and techniques for applying each strategy but also guiding principles that you and your colleagues can use as "touchstones" for making each strategy work in your classroom and for your students.

Using the strategies for instructional design and delivery

These strategies are, of course, most likely to stick when you build them into the design and delivery of every lesson and unit of study. Doing so will also help you integrate these strategies together into a powerful "bundle" of proven teaching techniques and effective learning opportunities for students—much like many of the interventions studied in the empirical research base for this book. Few, if any, were stand-alone strategies. Rather, they were incorporated into a larger set of strategies that, together, had powerful effects on student learning.

Throughout this book, we've noted that some of these strategies are designed to support *declarative knowledge* (content-based learning) and others to support *procedural knowledge* (skills-based learning). And some strategies support both. Figure 7.2 depicts how to weave these strategies together into teaching and learning pathways that support both declarative and procedural knowledge.

FIGURE 7.2   INSTRUCTIONAL PATHWAYS FOR DECLARATIVE
AND PROCEDURAL KNOWLEDGE

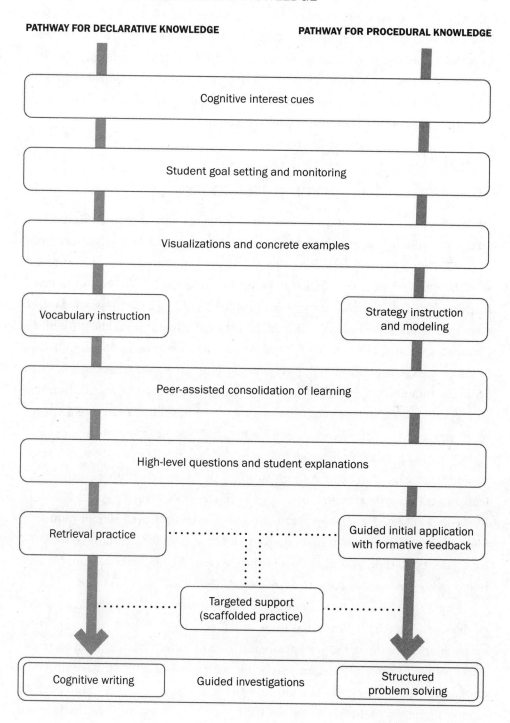

As you can see, some strategies (e.g., cognitive interest cues, student goal setting, and peer-assisted consolidation of learning) support both types of learning, whereas others are more suited to declarative knowledge (e.g., vocabulary instruction, cognitive writing) or procedural knowledge (e.g., strategy instruction and modeling, guided initial application with formative feedback). The key takeaway here is that you needn't use each strategy with every lesson or even unit. Rather, you should apply the strategies that are most suited to the learning at hand and that best address your students' learning needs.

Final Thoughts: The Power of Great Instruction for Diverse Learners

In this book we've identified 14 teaching strategies with demonstrated effect sizes equivalent to raising the achievement of average students anywhere from 10 to nearly 50 percentile points. It is worth noting that, depending on grade level, these effect sizes translate into several months if not a full year or more of learning (see, for example, Lipsey et al., 2012, for guidance on translating effect sizes into grade-level equivalents). Such powerful effects should be difficult to ignore—especially when the majority of the over 100 studies in our sample (see the Appendix) were conducted in classrooms with diverse learners, students in poverty, students with prior low achievement, and emergent bilingual students. In several studies, these practices were shown to narrow if not close achievement gaps and thus ensure more equitable outcomes for every learner.

Collectively, these findings should provide some inspiration; they offer reassurance that what you do in your classroom can make a difference in students' learning trajectories. Indeed, perhaps the biggest takeaway from this book is that you don't need whiz-bang technology, hypercomplicated school improvement plans, or the latest reform du jour to support more equitable outcomes for students. Rather, you can support the success of each and every learner by building proven teaching practices into every lesson and unit of study.

Finally, we hope this book unequivocally demonstrates that teaching *is* a profession—one that's grounded in as much science, research, and expertise as medicine, engineering, jurisprudence, or any other professional pursuit. Perhaps most important, when you bring evidence-based practices into your classroom, you can achieve the purpose that drew you into this noble profession: changing students' lives by ensuring they have opportunities to flourish in school and life.

Appendix:
Research Studies Supporting
The New Classroom
Instruction That Works

Summaries of these studies are available online at www.ascd.org/TheNewCITW.

FIGURE A.1   STRATEGY 1 SUPPORT: EMPIRICAL STUDIES OF COGNITIVE INTEREST CUES

Study	Treatment	n	Imp index	Grade level				Subject area				Student population			
				ES	MS	HS	Uni	ELA	Math	Sci	SS	>40% BIPOC	EL	LD	>40% FRL
Anand & Ross, 1987	Personalized vs. contextualized vs. abstract math problems	48	44	x					x			x			
August et al., 2009	Cognitive interest cues + vocabulary instruction + strategy instruction + visualizations + guided investigations	890	11		x					x		x	x		x
Bottge et al., 2002	Cognitive interest cues + visualizations + structured problem solving vs. traditional word problems	42	26		x				x					x	
Bottge et al., 2014	Cognitive interest cues + strategy instruction + structured problem solving vs. business-as-usual instruction	335	26		x				x					x	
Bottge et al., 2015	Cognitive interest cues + strategy instruction + structured problem solving vs. strategy instruction	417	25		x				x					x	
Cordova & Lepper, 1996	Cognitive interest cues (fantasy + personalization + choice) for math learning	70	49	x					x						
Dombek et al., 2017	Cognitive interest cues + guided investigations + cognitive writing	418	49	x						x	x	x			x
Guthrie et al., 2004	Cognitive interest cues + student goal setting + strategy instruction + peer-assisted consolidation + guided vs. strategy instruction only	361	26	x				x		x					
Guthrie et al., 2006	Stimulating science lessons (cognitive interest cues + high-level questions + guided investigations) vs. business-as-usual science lesson	98	26	x						x					x
Hulleman et al., 2010	Cognitive interest cues through reflective writing	318	10				x			x					
Kim et al., 2017	Cognitive interest cues + strategy instruction + peer-assisted consolidation	402	8		x			x			x	x		x	x
Lynch et al., 2007	Cognitive interest cues + guided inquiry vs. business-as-usual instruction	2,282	10		x					x		x		x	
Stevens, 2003	Cognitive interest cues + strategy instruction + peer-assisted consolidation + cognitive writing	3,916	10		x			x				x			x
Vaughn et al., 2017	Cognitive interest cues + vocabulary instruction + retrieval practice + peer-assisted consolidation + structured problem solving	1,629	16		x						x	x	x		x

Note: BIPOC = Black, Indigenous, and people of color; EL = English learners; ELA = English language arts; ES = elementary school; FRL = students receiving free and reduced-price lunch; HS = high school; Imp index = improvement index; LD = students with learning disabilities; MS = middle school; Sci = science; SS = social studies; Uni = university

FIGURE A.2   STRATEGY 2 SUPPORT: EMPIRICAL STUDIES OF STUDENT GOAL SETTING AND MONITORING

Study	Treatment	n	Imp index	Grade level				Subject area				Student population			
				ES	MS	HS	Uni	ELA	Math	Sci	SS	>40% BIPOC	EL	LD	>40% FRL
Blackwell et al., 2007	Teaching growth mindset + student goal setting	99	28		x				x			x			
Fuchs et al., 1997	Student goal setting (task-specific goals)	160	16	x					x			x		x	x
Fuchs et al., 2003	Student goal setting + self-monitoring	395	23	x					x			x			x
Glaser & Brunstein, 2007	Student goal setting + self-monitoring	113	26	x				x							
Graham et al., 1995	General vs. specific student goal setting for story writing	67	29	x				x						x	
Guthrie et al., 2004	Cognitive interest cues + student goal setting + strategy instruction + peer-assisted consolidation + guided initial instruction vs. strategy instruction only	361	26	x				x		x					
Limpo & Alves, 2014	Student goal setting + self-monitoring + strategy instruction	213	26	x				x							
Midgette et al., 2008	General vs. content vs. content + audience awareness student goal setting for persuasive writing	181	19	x	x			x							
Morisano et al., 2010	Visualize success + personal goals	84	26				x	x	x	x	x				
Olson et al., 2012	Direct instruction in thinking skills (including goal setting and asking questions) for writing	1,671	25		x	X		x				x	x		x
Olson et al., 2017	Direct instruction in thinking skills (including goal setting and asking questions) for writing	1,817	23		x	X		x				x	x		x
Page-Voth & Graham, 1999	Individual goal setting to improve persuasive writing	30	46		x			x						x	
Sawyer et al., 1992	Strategy instruction + goal setting and self-monitoring vs. strategy instruction alone	43	30	x				x				x		x	
Schunk & Swartz, 1991	Process goals vs. product goals	60	40	x				x							
Schunk & Swartz, 1993	Process goals + feedback vs. process goals alone	40	39	x				x				x			
Troia & Graham, 2002	Student goal setting + strategy instruction and modeling	24	47	x				x						x	

Note: BIPOC = Black, Indigenous, and people of color; EL = English learners; ELA = English language arts; ES = elementary school; FRL = students receiving free and reduced-price lunch; HS = high school; Imp index = improvement index; LD = students with learning disabilities; MS = middle school; Sci = science; SS = social studies; Uni = university

FIGURE A.3   STRATEGY 3 SUPPORT: EMPIRICAL STUDIES OF VOCABULARY INSTRUCTION

Study	Treatment	n	Imp index	Grade level				Subject area				Student population			
				ES	MS	HS	Uni	ELA	Math	Sci	SS	>40% BIPOC	EL	LD	>40% FRL
August et al., 2009	Vocabulary + cognitive interest cues + visual representations + guided discovery	890	11		x					x		x	x		x
Brown et al., 2010	Using everyday language to scaffold vocabulary instruction	49	32	x						x		x	x		x
Carlo et al., 2004	Strategy instruction in word skills + direct vocabulary instruction + peer-assisted consolidation	254	13	x				x				x	x		x
Fuchs, Schumacher, et al., 2013	Vocabulary instruction + strategy instruction + visualizations of math problems + retrieval practice + targeted supports	259	24	x					x			x		x	
Fuchs et al., 2021	Vocabulary instruction + structured problem solving (schema-based instruction)	391	46	x					x			x	x	x	x
Justice et al., 2005	Vocabulary instruction (elaboration of new words during storybook reading)	57	39	x				x				x	x		x
Lesaux et al., 2014	Direct instruction of academic vocabulary words	3,551	16		x			x			x	x	x		x
McKeown et al., 2018	Direct instruction of cross-curricular academic vocabulary	192	35		x			x	x	x	x				x
Tong et al., 2014	Academic vocabulary instruction + inquiry-based science + reading and writing strategy instruction	288	43		x			x		x		x			x
Townsend & Collins, 2009	After-school academic vocabulary instruction	37	32		x			x					x		
Vadasy et al., 2015	In-class vocabulary instruction for middle school students	1,232	11		x			x							
Vaughn et al., 2017	Cognitive interest cues + vocabulary instruction + strategy instruction + retrieval practice + team-based learning	1,629	16		x						x		x		
Wasik & Bond, 2001	Vocabulary instruction + visualizations and concrete objects	127	39	x				x				x		x	x
Wood et al., 2018	eBook vocabulary instruction for EL students	288	15	x				x				x	x		x

Note: BIPOC = Black, Indigenous, and people of color; EL = English learners; ELA = English language arts; ES = elementary school; FRL = students receiving free and reduced-price lunch; HS = high school; Imp index = improvement index; LD = students with learning disabilities; MS = middle school; Sci = science; SS = social studies; Uni = university

FIGURE A.4   STRATEGY 4 SUPPORT: EMPIRICAL STUDIES OF STRATEGY INSTRUCTION AND MODELING

Study	Treatment	n	Imp index	ES	MS	HS	Uni	ELA	Math	Sci	SS	>40% BIPOC	EL	LD	>40% FRL
				Grade level				Subject area				Student population			
August et al., 2009	Vocabulary + cognitive interest cues + strategy instruction + visualizations + guided investigation	890	11		x					x		x	x		x
Carlo et al., 2004	Strategy instruction in word skills + vocabulary instruction + peer-assisted consolidation	254	13	x				x				x	x		x
Fuchs, Schumacher, et al., 2013	Vocabulary instruction + strategy instruction + visualizations of math problems + retrieval practice + targeted supports	259	24	x					x			x		x	
Guthrie et al., 2004	Cognitive interest cues + student goal setting + strategy instruction + visualizations + high-level questions + peer-assisted consolidation + guided investigations vs. business-as-usual instruction	491	26	x						x		x			
Kim et al., 2011	Strategy instruction in writing + cognitive writing	1,393	14		x	x		x				x	x		x
Kim et al., 2017	Cue cognitive interest + strategy instruction + peer-assisted learning	402	8		x			x			x	x			x
Limpo & Alves, 2014	Goal setting + self-monitoring + strategy instruction	213	26	x				x							
Nelson et al., 2011	Phonics strategy instruction + targeted supports for EL students	185	35	x				x				x	x		x
Olson et al., 2012	Direct instruction of cognitive strategies for writing	1,671	25		x	x		x				x	x		x
Olson et al., 2017	Direct instruction of cognitive strategies for writing	1,817	23		x	x		x				x	x		x
Peng & Fuchs, 2017	Working memory training to support guided initial application	58	24	x					x			x		x	x
Saddler & Graham, 2005	Direct instruction in writing skills + peer-assisted learning	44	24	x				x							
Stevens, 2003	High-interest text + direct instruction of reading and writing strategies + frequent writing + peer-assisted learning	3,916	10		x			x				x			x
Tournaki, 2003	Strategy instruction vs. drill-and-practice vs. business-as-usual	84	43	x					x					x	
Troia & Graham, 2002	Direct instruction in goal setting + brainstorming + organizing	24	47	x				x						x	
Vadasy & Sanders, 2008	Supplemental strategy instruction in phonics + guided practice (individually and in dyads)	76	24	x				x				x		x	x
Vadasy & Sanders, 2010	Supplemental strategy instruction in phonics + guided practice (individually and in dyads)	148	30	x				x				x	x		x
Vaughn et al., 2006	Small-group strategy instruction in reading skills with guided practice in reading and writing	171	16	x				x				x	x		
Vaughn et al., 2017	Cognitive interest cues + vocabulary instruction + strategy instruction + retrieval practice + peer-assisted consolidation + problem solving	1,629	16		x						x		x		
Williams et al., 2007	Structure strategy instruction + high-level (cause-effect) questions for reading social studies texts	243	44	x				x			x			x	
Williams et al., 2014	Structure strategy instruction + high-level (cause-effect) questions for reading social studies texts	197	47	x				x			x	x			x
Woodward, 2006	Strategy instruction with interleaved practice vs. massed practice only	58	22	x					x					x	

Note: BIPOC = Black, Indigenous, and people of color; EL = English learners; ELA = English language arts; ES = elementary school; FRL = students receiving free and reduced-price lunch; HS = high school; Imp index = improvement index; LD = students with learning disabilities; MS = middle school; Sci = science; SS = social studies; Uni = university

FIGURE A.5   STRATEGY 5 SUPPORT: EMPIRICAL STUDIES OF VISUALIZATIONS AND CONCRETE EXAMPLES

Study	Treatment	n	Imp index	Grade level				Subject area				Student population			
				ES	MS	HS	Uni	ELA	Math	Sci	SS	>40% BIPOC	EL	LD	>40% FRL
August et al., 2009	Vocabulary + cognitive interest cues + visualizations + guided discovery	890	11		x					x		x	x		x
Bottge et al., 2002	Manipulatives + hands-on learning to visualize math concepts	42	26		x				x					x	
Bottge et al., 2014	Cognitive interest cues + strategy instruction + structured problem solving vs. business-as-usual instruction	335	26		x				x					x	
Bulgren et al., 2000	Anchoring math learning in concrete representations	83	34			x				x	x				
Fuchs, Schumacher, et al., 2013	Vocabulary instruction + strategy instruction + visualizations of math problems + retrieval practice + targeted supports	259	24	x					x			x	x		
Guthrie et al., 2004	Cognitive interest cues + student goal setting + strategy instruction + visualizations + high-level questions + peer-assisted consolidation + guided investigations vs. business-as-usual instruction	491	26	x						x		x			
Ives, 2007	Graphic organizers + strategy instruction	30	42		x	x			x					x	
Jitendra et al., 2009	Tutoring in schema-based instruction + visualizations + student explanations	148	21		x				x			x			x
Jitendra et al., 2011	Schema-based instruction (visualizations + structured problem solving)	436	27		x				x			x			x
Jitendra et al., 2013	Tutoring in schema-based instruction (visualizations + structured problem solving) vs. tutoring in computational skills	109	18	x					x			x	x	x	x
Kalyuga et al., 2001	Worked-out examples vs. exploratory learning for complex tasks	17	24				x		x						
Mwangi & Sweller, 1998	Step-by-step worked examples for solving math problems	27	44	x					x						
Outhwaite et al., 2019	Visually rich, direct instruction + play-based retrieval practice	389	12	x					x						
Rittle-Johnson & Star, 2007	Comparing worked-out examples of different solution methods simultaneously vs. sequentially	70	20		x				x						
Roschelle et al., 2010	Visual representations + interactive manipulatives + student explanations	825	21		x				x						
Scheiter et al., 2010	Visual representations + worked-out examples	32	37		x				x						
Silverman & Hines, 2009	Video clips to aid academic vocabulary acquisition	85	33	x						x			x		
Star & Rittle-Johnson, 2009	Comparing worked-out examples of different solution methods simultaneously vs. sequentially	157	11	x					x						
Swanson et al., 2013	Visual-schematic instruction	120	22	x					x					x	
Terwel et al., 2009	Student-created visual representations	239	24	x					x						
Wasik & Bond, 2001	Interactive book reading with concrete objects to increase pre-K vocabulary	127	39	x				x				x		x	x
Xin et al., 2005	Schema-based instruction + schematic diagrams vs. general strategy instruction	22	45		x				x			x		x	
Zhou & Yadav, 2017	Multimedia stories with animations and interactive definitions of new words	72	9	x				x							

Note: BIPOC = Black, Indigenous, and people of color; EL = English learners; ELA = English language arts; ES = elementary school; FRL = students receiving free and reduced-price lunch; HS = high school; Imp index = improvement index; LD = students with learning disabilities; MS = middle school; Sci = science; SS = social studies; Uni = university

FIGURE A.6   STRATEGY 6 SUPPORT: EMPIRICAL STUDIES OF HIGH-LEVEL QUESTIONS AND STUDENT EXPLANATIONS

Study	Treatment	n	Imp index	Grade level				Subject area				Student population			
				ES	MS	HS	Uni	ELA	Math	Sci	SS	>40% BIPOC	EL	LD	>40% FRL
Clariana & Koul, 2006	Text with delayed feedback on high-level questions vs. text with no questions	82	34			x			x						
Fuchs et al., 2014	Small-group instruction with student self-explaining vs. business-as-usual control	243	37	x					x			x		x	x
Fuchs et al., 2016	Supported self-explaining vs. word-problem practice	212	42	x					x			x		x	x
Guthrie et al., 2004	Cognitive interest cues + student goal setting + strategy instruction + visualizations + high-level questions + peer-assisted consolidation + guided investigations vs. business-as-usual instruction	491	26	x						x		x			
Guthrie et al., 2006	High-stimulation learning activities (cognitive interest cues + high-level questions + guided investigations) vs. business-as-usual instruction	98	26	x						x					x
Jitendra et al., 2009	Tutoring in schema-based instruction + visualizations + student explanations	148	21		x				x			x			x
King, 1991	Guided questions vs. unguided questions vs. no questions	46	34	x											
Kramarski & Mevarech, 2003	Metacognitive questions + peer-assisted consolidation of learning	384	28		x				x						
McDougall & Granby, 1996	Random cold calling vs. voluntary response	40	36				x		x						
Olson et al., 2012	Direct instruction in thinking skills (including goal setting and asking questions) for writing	1,671	25		x	x		x				x	x		x
Olson et al., 2017	Direct instruction in thinking skills (including goal setting and asking questions) for writing	1,817	23		x	x		x				x	x		x
Roschelle et al., 2010	Visual representations + interactive manipulatives + student explanations	825	21		x				x						
Scruggs et al., 1994	Student self-explanations vs. provided explanations vs. repetition	36	30	x						x				x	
Tajika et al., 2007	Think-aloud vs. independent practice for solving word problems	79	32		x				x						
Williams et al., 2007	Structure strategy instruction + high-level (cause-effect) questions for reading social studies texts	243	44	x				x			x			x	
Williams et al., 2014	Structure strategy instruction + high-level (cause-effect) questions for reading social studies texts	197	47	x				x			x	x			x
Zhou & Yadav, 2017	Open-ended processing questions during reading	72	18	x				x							

Note: BIPOC = Black, Indigenous, and people of color; EL = English learners; ELA = English language arts; ES = elementary school; FRL = students receiving free and reduced-price lunch; HS = high school; Imp index = improvement index; LD = students with learning disabilities; MS = middle school; Sci = science; SS = social studies; Uni = university.

FIGURE A.7   STRATEGY 7 SUPPORT: EMPIRICAL STUDIES OF GUIDED INITIAL APPLICATION WITH FORMATIVE FEEDBACK

Study	Treatment	n	Imp index	Grade level				Subject area				Student population			
				ES	MS	HS	Uni	ELA	Math	Sci	SS	>40% BIPOC	EL	LD	>40% FRL
Cardelle-Elawar, 1990	Guided practice with metacognitive strategies and descriptive feedback	80	49		x				x			x	x		x
Dyson et al., 2015	Targeted supports for math + guided initial application + number-fact retrieval practice	276	29	x					x			x	x		x
Fuchs, Fuchs, et al., 2008	Schema-broadening instruction + guided initial application + targeted support	243	38	x					x			x			x
Fuchs et al., 2009	Guided practice tutoring for word problem solving vs. no-tutoring control	133	29	x					x			x		x	x
Fuchs et al., 2010	Tutoring with deliberate practice	180	23	x					x			x			x
Fuchs, Geary, et al., 2013	Tutoring with nonspeeded conceptual guidance (guided practice) vs. no-tutoring control (complex calculations)	591	19	x					x			x		x	x
Powell et al., 2009	Tutoring with formative feedback during fact-retrieval practice	139	19	20					x			x		x	x
Roschelle et al., 2016	Online guided and spaced practice with immediate feedback	2,850	11		x				x						
Vadasy & Sanders, 2008	Supplemental strategy instruction in phonics + guided practice (individually and in dyads)	76	24	x				x				x		x	x
Vadasy & Sanders, 2010	Supplemental strategy instruction in phonics + guided practice (individually and in dyads)	148	30	x				x				x	x		x
Vaughn et al., 2006	Small-group strategy instruction in reading skills with guided practice in reading and writing	171	16	x				x				x	x		

Note: BIPOC = Black, Indigenous, and people of color; EL = English learners; ELA = English language arts; ES = elementary school; FRL = students receiving free and reduced-price lunch; HS = high school; Imp index = improvement index; LD = students with learning disabilities; MS = middle school; Sci = science; SS = social studies; Uni = university

FIGURE A.8   STRATEGY 8 SUPPORT: EMPIRICAL STUDIES OF PEER-ASSISTED CONSOLIDATION OF LEARNING

Study	Treatment	n	Imp index	Grade level				Subject area				Student population			
				ES	MS	HS	Uni	ELA	Math	Sci	SS	>40% BIPOC	EL	LD	>40% FRL
Carlo et al., 2004	Strategy instruction in word skills + direct vocabulary instruction + peer-assisted consolidation	254	13	x				x				x	x		x
Guthrie et al., 2004	Cognitive interest cues + student goal setting + strategy instruction + visualizations + high-level questions + peer-assisted consolidation + guided investigations vs. business-as-usual instruction	491	42	x						x		x			
Kim et al., 2017	Cue cognitive interest + strategy instruction + peer-assisted learning	402	8		x			x			x				x
Kramarski & Mevarech, 2003	Peer-assisted processing of metacognitive questions	384	28		x				x						
Saddler & Graham, 2005	Direct instruction in writing skills + peer-assisted learning	44	24	x				x							
Stevens, 2003	High-interest text + strategy instruction + cognitive writing + peer-assisted consolidation	3,916	10		x			x				x			x
Tong et al., 2014	Vocabulary instruction + peer-assisted consolidation + inquiry-based science + cognitive writing	288	43		x			x		x		x			x
Vaughn et al., 2017	Cognitive interest cues + vocabulary instruction + strategy instruction + retrieval practice + team-based problem solving	1,629	16		x						x		x		
Wanzek et al., 2014	Team-based learning vs. whole-class and independent work	432	9			x					x	x			

Note: BIPOC = Black, Indigenous, and people of color; EL = English learners; ELA = English language arts; ES = elementary school; FRL = students receiving free and reduced-price lunch; HS = high school; Imp index = improvement index; LD = students with learning disabilities; MS = middle school; Sci = science; SS = social studies; Uni = university

FIGURE A.9   STRATEGY 9 SUPPORT: EMPIRICAL STUDIES OF RETRIEVAL PRACTICE (QUIZZING TO REMEMBER)

Study	Treatment	n	Imp index	Grade level				Subject area				Student population			
				ES	MS	HS	Uni	ELA	Math	Sci	SS	>40% BIPOC	EL	LD	>40% FRL
Carpenter et al., 2009	Retrieval practice vs. studying	75	13		x						x				
Dyson et al., 2015	Targeted intervention for math procedural knowledge + number-fact practice	276	29	x					x			x	x		x
Fuchs et al., 2009	Retrieval practice tutoring vs. no-tutoring control	133	21	x					x			x		x	x
Fuchs, Geary, et al., 2013	Tutoring speeded retrieval practice with feedback vs. no-tutoring control (complex calculations)	591	26	x					x			x		x	x
Fuchs, Schumacher, et al., 2013	Small-group tutoring with visualizations + strategy instruction + vocabulary + retrieval practice	259	24	x					x			x		x	x
Fuchs et al., 2014	Small group speeded retrieval practice vs. business-as-usual instruction	243	37	x					x			x		x	x
Karpicke & Blunt, 2011	Retrieval practice v. elaborative studying	120	36			x				x					
Karpicke & Smith, 2012	Repeated retrieval vs. repeated studying	90	11			x				x					
Outhwaite et al., 2019	Visually rich, direct instruction + play-based retrieval practice	389	12	x					x						
Powell et al., 2009	Tutoring with corrective feedback during fact-retrieval practice	139	19	x					x			x		x	x
Rawson & Dunlosky, 2011	Repeated retrieval sessions—three vs. one	335	33			x				x					

Note: BIPOC = Black, Indigenous, and people of color; EL = English learners; ELA = English language arts; ES = elementary school; FRL = students receiving free and reduced-price lunch; HS = high school; Imp index = improvement index; LD = students with learning disabilities; MS = middle school; Sci = science; SS = social studies; Uni = university

FIGURE A.10 STRATEGY 10 SUPPORT: EMPIRICAL STUDIES OF INTERLEAVED, SPACED INDEPENDENT PRACTICE

Study	Treatment	n	Imp index	Grade level				Subject area				Student population			
				ES	MS	HS	Uni	ELA	Math	Sci	SS	>40% BIPOC	EL	LD	>40% FRL
Mayfield & Chase, 2002	Interleaving practice vs. massed practice with algebra problems	33	47	x			x		x						
McNeil et al., 2011	Practice with nontraditional presentation of math problems	90	28	x					x						
Powell et al., 2015	Interleaved practice with nonstandard and standard equations	51	24	x					x			x			x
Rohrer et al., 2014	Interleaved practice in mathematics	140	35		x				x						
Rohrer et al., 2020	Interleaved practice in mathematics	54	30	x					x						
Roschelle et al., 2016	Online guided and spaced practice with feedback	2,850	9		x				x						
Woodward, 2006	Strategy instruction with interleaved practice vs. massed practice only	58	22	x					x					x	

Note: BIPOC = Black, Indigenous, and people of color; EL = English learners; ELA = English language arts; ES = elementary school; FRL = students receiving free and reduced-price lunch; HS = high school; Imp index = improvement index; LD = students with learning disabilities; MS = middle school; Sci = science; SS = social studies; Uni = university

FIGURE A.11   STRATEGY 11 SUPPORT: EMPIRICAL STUDIES OF TARGETED SUPPORT (SCAFFOLDED PRACTICE)

Study	Treatment	n	Imp index	Grade level				Subject area				Student population			
				ES	MS	HS	Uni	ELA	Math	Sci	SS	>40% BIPOC	EL	LD	>40% FRL
Connor et al., 2011	1 year of targeted reading instruction	396	19	x				x				x			x
Connor et al., 2013	3 years of targeted reading instruction	357	17	x				x							x
Coyne et al., 2019	Tier 2 vocabulary instruction for at-risk students	2,347	36	x				x				x		x	
Doabler et al., 2016	Tier 2 supports for students experiencing math difficulties	316	12	x				x				x		x	x
Dyson et al., 2015	Targeted supports for math + guided initial application + number-fact retrieval practice	276	29	x					x			x	x		x
Fuchs, Fuchs, et al., 2008	Small-group tutoring in schema-broadening instruction	243	38	x					x			x			x
Fuchs et al., 2009	Guided practice tutoring for word problem solving vs. no-tutoring control	133	29	x					x			x		x	x
Fuchs et al., 2010	Tutoring with and without deliberate practice and reflective feedback	180	23	x					x			x			x
Fuchs, Geary, et al., 2013	Tutoring with nonspeeded conceptual guidance (guided practice) vs. no-tutoring control (complex calculations)	591	19	x					x			x		x	x
Fuchs, Schumacher, et al., 2013	Small-group tutoring with visualizations + strategy instruction + vocabulary + retrieval practice	259	24	x					x			x		x	x
Fuchs et al., 2014	Small-group tutoring with student self-explanation or speeded retrieval practice	243	37	x					x			x		x	x
Nelson et al., 2011	Phonics strategy instruction + targeted supports for EL students	185	35	x				x				x	x		x
Pullen et al., 2010	Targeted support for vocabulary acquisition	224	24	x				x				x	x		x
Vadasy & Sanders, 2008	Student tutoring in decoding (individually and in dyads)	76	24	x				x				x		x	x
Vadasy & Sanders, 2010	Supplemental phonics instruction and guided practice	148	30	x				x				x	x		x
Vaughn et al., 2006	Phonics-based, small-group reading instruction with guided practice in reading and writing	171	16	x				x				x	x		
Vaughn et al., 2017	Cognitive interest cues + vocabulary instruction + strategy instruction + retrieval practice + team-based learning	1,629	16		x						x		x		

Note: BIPOC = Black, Indigenous, and people of color; EL = English learners; ELA = English language arts; ES = elementary school; FRL = students receiving free and reduced-price lunch; HS = high school; Imp index = improvement index; LD = students with learning disabilities; MS = middle school; Sci = science; SS = social studies; Uni = university

FIGURE A.12   STRATEGY 12 SUPPORT: EMPIRICAL STUDIES OF COGNITIVE WRITING

Study	Treatment	n	Imp index	Grade level				Subject area				Student population			
				ES	MS	HS	Uni	ELA	Math	Sci	SS	>40% BIPOC	EL	LD	>40% FRL
Collins et al., 2017	Visualizations (thinksheets) to support cognitive writing vs. business-as-usual instruction	1,062	19	x				x				x			x
Dombek et al., 2017	Cognitive interest cues + reading + experiments + cognitive writing	418	49	x						x	x	x			x
Kim et al., 2011	Strategy instruction in writing + cognitive writing	1,393	14		x	x		x				x	x		x
Olson et al., 2012	Direct instruction of cognitive strategies for writing	1,671	25		x	x		x				x	x		x
Olson et al., 2017	Direct instruction of cognitive strategies for writing	1,817	23		x	x		x				x	x		x
Stevens, 2003	High-interest text + direct instruction of reading and writing strategies + peer-assisted consolidation + cognitive writing	3,916	10		x			x				x			x
Tong et al., 2014	Vocabulary instruction + peer-assisted consolidation + inquiry-based science + cognitive writing	288	43		x			x		x		x			x

Note: BIPOC = Black, Indigenous, and people of color; EL = English learners; ELA = English language arts; ES = elementary school; FRL = students receiving free and reduced-price lunch; HS = high school; Imp index = improvement index; LD = students with learning disabilities; MS = middle school; Sci = science; SS = social studies; Uni = university

FIGURE A.13   STRATEGY 13 SUPPORT: EMPIRICAL STUDIES OF GUIDED INVESTIGATIONS

Study	Treatment	n	Imp index	Grade level				Subject area				Student population			
				ES	MS	HS	Uni	ELA	Math	Sci	SS	>40% BIPOC	EL	LD	>40% FRL
August et al., 2009	Vocabulary + cognitive interest cues + visual representations + guided investigation	890	11		x			x		x		x	x		x
Dombek et al., 2017	Cognitive interest cues + reading + guided experiments + writing in response to open-ended questions	418	49	x						x	x	x			x
Friedman et al., 2017	Formal direct instruction + guided inquiry vs. business-as-usual instruction	1,166	15		x					x		x			x
Guthrie et al., 2004	Cognitive interest cues + goal setting + strategy instruction + visualizations + high-level questions + peer-assisted consolidation + guided investigations	491	26	x						x		x			
Guthrie et al., 2006	High-stimulation learning activities (cognitive interest cues + high-level questions + guided investigations) vs. business-as-usual instruction	98	26	x						x					x
Lorch et al., 2010	Explicit instruction + experimentation vs. experimentation only	460	27	x						x					x
Lynch et al., 2007	Cognitive interest cues + guided inquiry vs. business-as-usual instruction	2,282	10		x					x		x		x	
Tong et al., 2014	Vocabulary instruction + peer-assisted consolidation + inquiry-based science + cognitive writing	288	43		x			x		x		x			x

Note: BIPOC = Black, Indigenous, and people of color; EL = English learners; ELA = English language arts; ES = elementary school; FRL = students receiving free and reduced-price lunch; HS = high school; Imp index = improvement index; LD = students with learning disabilities; MS = middle school; Sci = science; SS = social studies; Uni = university

FIGURE A.14   STRATEGY 14 SUPPORT: EMPIRICAL STUDIES OF STRUCTURED PROBLEM SOLVING

Study	Treatment	n	Imp index	Grade level				Subject area				Student population			
				ES	MS	HS	Uni	ELA	Math	Sci	SS	>40% BIPOC	EL	LD	>40% FRL
Bottge et al., 2002	Cognitive interest cues + visualizations + structured problem solving vs. traditional word problems	42	26		x				x					x	
Bottge et al., 2014	Cognitive interest cues + strategy instruction + structured problem solving vs. business-as-usual instruction	335	26		x				x					x	
Bottge et al., 2015	Cognitive interest cues + strategy instruction + structured problem solving vs. procedural instruction on abstract problems	417	25		x				x					x	
Fuchs et al., 2004	Expanded strategy-based transfer instruction vs. business-as-usual classroom instruction	351	47	x					x			x			x
Fuchs, Fuchs, et al., 2008	Schema-broadening instruction + guided initial application + targeted support	243	38	x					x			x			x
Fuchs et al., 2009	Tutoring focused on word problem skills vs. number combination skills	133	29	x					x			x		x	x
Fuchs et al., 2021	Vocabulary instruction + schema-based instruction for word problem solving	391	46	x					x			x	x	x	x
Jitendra et al., 2009	Tutoring in schema-based instruction + visualizations + student explanations	148	21		x				x			x			x
Jitendra et al., 2011	Schema-based instruction (visualizations + structured problem solving)	436	27		x				x			x			x
Jitendra et al., 2013	Tutoring in schema-based instruction (visualizations + structured problem solving) vs. tutoring in computational skills	109	18	x					x			x	x	x	x
Vaughn et al., 2017	Cognitive interest cues + vocabulary instruction + strategy instruction + retrieval practice + team-based problem solving	1,629	16		x						x	x			
Xin et al., 2005	Schema-based instruction + schematic diagrams vs. general strategy instruction	22	45		x				x			x		x	

Note: BIPOC = Black, Indigenous, and people of color; EL = English learners; ELA = English language arts; ES = elementary school; FRL = students receiving free and reduced-price lunch; HS = high school; Imp index = improvement index; LD = students with learning disabilities; MS = middle school; Sci = science; SS = social studies; Uni = university

References

Note: Studies included in the synthesis are in **bold type.**

Abrami, P. C., Bernard, R. M., Borokhovski, E., Waddington, D. I., Wade, C. A., & Persson, T. (2015). Strategies for teaching students to think critically: A meta-analysis. *Review of Educational Research, 85*(2), 275–314. https://doi.org/10.3102/0034654314551063

Alfieri, L., Brooks, P. J., Aldrich, N. J., & Tenenbaum, H. R. (2011). Does discovery-based instruction enhance learning? *Journal of Educational Psychology, 103*(1), 1. https://doi.org/10.1037/a0021017

Anand, P. G., & Ross, S. M. (1987). Using computer-assisted instruction to personalize arithmetic materials for elementary school children. ***Journal of Educational Psychology, 79***(1)**, 72–78. https://doi.org/10.1037/0022-0663.79.1.72**

Anderson, J. R. (1995). *Learning and memory: An integrated approach.* Wiley.

August, D., Branum-Martin, L., Cardenas-Hagan, E., & Francis, D. J. (2009). The impact of an instructional intervention on the science and language learning of middle grade English language learners. ***Journal of Research on Educational Effectiveness, 2***(4)**, 345–376. https://doi.org/10.1080/19345740903217623**

Bailey, F., & Pransky, K. (2014). *Memory at work in the classroom: Strategies to help underachieving students.* ASCD.

Bandura, A., & Schunk, D. H. (1981). Cultivating competence, self-efficacy, and intrinsic interest through proximal self-motivation. *Journal of Personality and Social Psychology, 41*(3), 586–598. https://psycnet.apa.org/doi/10.1037/0022-3514.41.3.586

Bangert-Drowns, R. L., & Bankert, E. (1990, April). *Meta-analysis of effects of explicit instruction for critical thinking.* Paper presented at American Educational Research Association Annual Meeting, Boston.

Beck, I. L., Perfetti, C. A., & McKeown, M. G. (1982). Effects of long-term vocabulary instruction on lexical access and reading comprehension. *Journal of Educational Psychology, 74*(4), 506–521. https://doi.org/10.1037/0022-0663.74.4.506

Beesley, A. D., & Apthorp, H. S. (2010). *Classroom instruction that works.* (Research report). Mid-continent Research for Education and Learning (McREL).

Berry, D. C. (1983). Metacognitive experience and transfer of logical reasoning. *The Quarterly Journal of Experimental Psychology Section A, 35*(1), 39–49. https://doi.org/10.1080/14640748308402115

Bjork, E. L., & Bjork, R. A. (2011). Making things hard on yourself, but in a good way: Creating desirable difficulties to enhance learning. In M. A. Gernsbacher, R. W. Pew, L. M. Hough, & J. R. Pomerantz (Eds.), *Psychology and the real world: Essays illustrating fundamental contributions to society* (pp. 56–64). Worth Publishers.

Bjork, R. A., & Bjork, E. L. (1992). A new theory of disuse and an old theory of stimulus fluctuation. In A. F. Healy, S. M. Kosslyn, & R. M. Shiffrin (Eds.), *From learning processes to cognitive processes: Essays in honor of William K. Estes* (Vol. 2., pp. 35–67). Lawrence Erlbaum Associates.

Blackwell, L. S., Trzesniewski, K. H., & Dweck, C. S. (2007). Implicit theories of intelligence predict achievement across an adolescent transition: A longitudinal study and an intervention. *Child Development, 78*(1), 246–263. https://doi.org/10.1111/j.1467-8624.2007.00995.x

Bloom, B. (1985). *Developing talent in young people.* Ballantine Books.

Bottge, B. A. (2001, March). Using intriguing problems to improve math skills. *Educational Leadership, 56*(6), 88–72.

Bottge, B. A., Heinrichs, M., Mehta, Z. D., & Hung, Y.-H. (2002). Weighing the benefits of anchored math instruction for students with disabilities in general education classes. *The Journal of Special Education, 35*(4), 186–200. https://doi.org/10.1177/002246690203500401

Bottge, B. A., Ma, X., Gassaway, L., Toland, M. D., Butler, M., & Cho, S.-J. (2014). Effects of blended instructional models on math performance. *Exceptional Children, 80*(4), 423–437. https://doi.org/10.1177/0014402914527240

Bottge, B. A., Toland, M. D., Gassaway, L., Butler, M., Choo, S., Griffen, A. K., & Ma, X. (2015). Impact of enhanced anchored instruction in inclusive math classrooms. *Exceptional Children, 81*(2), 158–175. https://doi.org/10.1177/0014402914551742

Brand-Gruwel, S., Wopereis, I., & Vermetten, Y. (2005). Information problem solving by experts and novices: Analysis of a complex cognitive skill. *Computers in Human Behavior, 21*(3), 487–508. https://doi.org/10.1016/j.chb.2004.10.005

Brophy, J. (2004). *Motivating students to learn.* Routledge. https://doi.org/10.4324/9781410610218

Brown, B. A., Ryoo, K., & Rodriguez, J. (2010). Pathway towards fluency: Using "disaggregate instruction" to promote science literacy. *International Journal of Science Education, 32*(11), 1465–1493. https://doi.org/10.1080/09500690903117921

Brown, P. C., Roediger, H. L., III, & McDaniel, M. A. (2014). *Make it stick: The science of successful learning.* Harvard University Press.

Bulgren, J. A., Deshler, D. D., Schumaker, J. B., & Lenz, B. K. (2000). The use and effectiveness of analogical instruction in diverse secondary content classrooms. *Journal of Educational Psychology, 92*(3), 426–441. https://doi.org/10.1037/0022-0663.92.3.426

Busteed, B. (2013, January 7). *The school cliff: Student engagement drops with each school year.* Gallup. https://news.gallup.com/opinion/gallup/170525/school-cliff-student-engagement-drops-school-year.aspx

Butler, A. C., & Roediger, H. L. (2008). Feedback enhances the positive effects and reduces the negative effects of multiple-choice testing. *Memory & Cognition, 36*(3), 604–616. https://doi.org/10.3758/MC.36.3.604

Cardelle-Elawar, M. (1990). Effects of feedback tailored to bilingual students' mathematics needs on verbal problem solving. *The Elementary School Journal, 91*(2), 165–175. https://doi.org/10.1086/461644

Carlo, M. S., August, D., McLaughlin, B., Snow, C. E., Dressler, C., Lippman, D. N., Lively, T. J., & White, C. E. (2004). Closing the gap: Addressing the vocabulary needs of English-language learners in bilingual and mainstream classrooms. *Reading Research Quarterly, 39*(2), 188–215. https://doi.org/10.1598/RRQ.39.2.3

Carpenter, S. K., Pashler, H., & Cepeda, N. J. (2009). Using tests to enhance 8th grade students' retention of U.S. history facts. *Applied Cognitive Psychology, 23*(6), 760–771. https://doi.org/10.1002/acp.1507

Cerasoli, C. P., Nicklin, J. M., & Ford, M. T. (2014). Intrinsic motivation and extrinsic incentives jointly predict performance: A 40-year meta-analysis. *Psychological Bulletin, 140*(4), 980–1008. https://doi.org/10.1037/a0035661

Chi, M. T., De Leeuw, N., Chiu, M. H., & LaVancher, C. (1994). Eliciting self-explanations improves understanding. *Cognitive Science, 18*(3), 439–477. https://doi.org/10.1207/s15516709cog1803_3

Cialdini, R. B. (2005). What's the best secret device for engaging student interest? The answer is in the title. *Journal of Social and Clinical Psychology, 24*(1), 22–29. https://doi.org/10.1521/jscp.24.1.22.59166

City, E. A., Elmore, R. F., Fiarman, S. E., & Teitel, L. (2009). *Instructional rounds in education* (Vol. 30). Harvard Education Press.

Clariana, R. B., & Koul, R. (2006). The effects of different forms of feedback on fuzzy and verbatim memory of science principles. *British Journal of Educational Psychology, 76*(2), 259–270. https://doi.org/10.1348/000709905X39134

Coleman, J. S. (1966). *Equality of educational opportunity study.* U.S. Department of Health, Education, and Welfare.

Collins, J. L., Lee, J., Fox, J. D., & Madigan, T. P. (2017). Bringing together reading and writing: An experimental study of writing intensive reading comprehension in low-performing urban elementary schools. *Reading Research Quarterly, 52*(3), 311–332. https://doi.org/10.1002/rrq.175

Connor, C. M., Morrison, F. J., Fishman, B., Crowe, E. C., Otaiba, S. A., & Schatschneider, C. (2013). A longitudinal cluster-randomized controlled study on the accumulating effects of individualized literacy instruction on students' reading from first through third grade. *Psychological Science, 24*(8), 1408–1419. https://doi.org/10.1177/0956797612472204

Connor, C. M., Morrison, F. J., Schatschneider, C., Toste, J. R., Lundblom, E., Crowe, E. C., & Fishman, B. (2011). Effective classroom instruction: Implications of child characteristics by reading instruction interactions on first graders' word reading achievement. *Journal of Research on Educational Effectiveness, 4*(3), 173–207. https://doi.org/10.1080/19345747.2010.510179

Cordova, D. I., & Lepper, M. R. (1996). Intrinsic motivation and the process of learning: Beneficial effects of contextualization, personalization, and choice. *Journal of Educational Psychology, 88*(4), 715–730. https://doi.org/10.1037/0022-0663.88.4.715

Coyne, M. D., McCoach, D. B., Ware, S., Austin, C. R., Loftus-Rattan, S. M., & Baker, D. L. (2019). Racing against the vocabulary gap: Matthew effects in early vocabulary instruction and intervention. *Exceptional Children, 85*(2), 163–179. https://doi.org/10.1177/0014402918789162

de Groot, A. (1966). Perception and memory versus thought: Some old ideas and recent findings. In B. Kleinmuntz (Ed.), *Problem solving* (pp. 19–50). Wiley.

Dean, C. B., Hubbell, E. R., Pitler, H., & Stone, B. J. (2012). *Classroom instruction that works: Research-based strategies for increasing student achievement* (2nd ed.). ASCD and McREL.

Deci, E. L., Ryan, R. M., & Koestner, R. (1999). A meta-analytic review of experiments examining the effects of extrinsic rewards on intrinsic motivation. *Psychological Bulletin, 125*(6), 627–668. https://doi.org/10.1037/0033-2909.125.6.627

Doabler, C. T., Clarke, B., Kosty, D. B., Kurtz-Nelson, E., Fien, H., Smolkowski, K., & Baker, S. K. (2016). Testing the efficacy of a Tier 2 mathematics intervention: A conceptual replication study. *Exceptional Children, 83*(1), 92–110. https://doi.org/10.1177/0014402916660084

Dombek, J., Crowe, E. C., Spencer, M., Tighe, E. L., Coffinger, S., Zargar, E., Wood, T., & Petscher, Y. (2017). Acquiring science and social studies knowledge in kindergarten through fourth grade: Conceptualization, design, implementation, and efficacy testing of content-area literacy instruction (CALI). *Journal of Educational Psychology, 109*(3), 301–320. https://doi.org/10.1037/edu0000128

Dweck, C. S. (2000). *Self theories: Their role in motivation, personality, and development.* Taylor & Francis.

Dweck, C. (2006). *Mindset: The new psychology of success.* Random House.

Dyson, N., Jordan, N. C., Beliakoff, A., & Hassinger-Das, B. (2015). A kindergarten number-sense intervention with contrasting practice conditions for low-achieving children. *Journal for Research in Mathematics Education, 46*(3), 331–370. https://doi.org/10.5951/jresematheduc.46.3.0331

Ebbinghaus, H. (1964). *Memory: A contribution to experimental psychology.* Dover. (Original work published 1885; translated 1913)

Ekstrom, R., Goertz, M., Pollack, J., & Rock, D. (1986). Who drops out of high school and why? Findings from a national study. *Teachers College Record, 87*(3), 356–373. https://doi .org/10.1177/016146818608700308

Finn, J. D., & Rock, D. A. (1997). Academic success among students at risk for school failure. *Journal of Applied Psychology, 82*(2), 221–234. https://doi.org/10.1037/0021-9010.82.2.221

Fisher, D., & Frey, N. (2021). *Better learning through structured teaching: A framework for the gradual release of responsibility* (3rd ed.). ASCD.

Frayer, D., Frederick, W. C., & Klausmeier, H. J. (1969). *A schema for testing the level of cognitive mastery.* Wisconsin Center for Education Research.

Friedman, L. B., Margolin, J., Swanlund, A., Dhillon, S., & Liu, F. (2017). *Enhancing middle school science lessons with playground activities: A study of the impact of playground physics.* American Institutes of Research. https://files.eric.ed.gov /fulltext/ED574773.pdf

Fritz, C. O., Morris, P. E., Nolan, D., & Singleton, J. (2007). Expanding retrieval practice: An effective aid to preschool children's learning. *Quarterly Journal of Experimental Psychology, 60*(7), 991–1004. https://doi.org/10.1080/17470210600823595

Fuchs, L. S., Fuchs, D., Craddock, C., Hollenbeck, K. N., Hamlett, C. L., & Schatschneider, C. (2008). Effects of small-group tutoring with and without validated classroom instruction on at-risk students' math problem solving: Are two tiers of prevention better than one? *Journal of Educational Psychology, 100*(3), 491–509. https://doi.org/10.1037/0022-0663.100.3.491

Fuchs, L. S., Fuchs, D., Finelli, R., Courey, S. J., & Hamlett, C. L. (2004). Expanding schema-based transfer instruction to help third graders solve real-life mathematical problems. *American Educational Research Journal, 41*(2), 419–445. https://doi.org/10.3102/00028312041002419

Fuchs, L. S., Fuchs, D., Karns, K., Hamlett, C. L., Katzaroff, M., & Dutka, S. (1997). Effects of task-focused goals on low-achieving students with and without learning disabilities. *American Educational Research Journal, 34*(3), 513–543. https:// doi.org/10.3102/00028312034003513

Fuchs, L. S., Fuchs, D., Prentice, K., Burch, M., Hamlett, C. L., Owen, R., & Schroeter, K. (2003). Enhancing third-grade students' mathematical problem solving with self-regulated learning strategies. *Journal of Educational Psychology, 95*(2), 306–315. https://doi.org/10.1037/0022-0663.95.2.306

Fuchs, L. S., Geary, D. C., Compton, D. L., Fuchs, D., Schatschneider, C., Hamlett, C. L., DeSelms, J., Seethaler, P. M., Wilson, J., Craddock, C. F., Bryant, J. D., Luther, K., & Changas, P. (2013). Effects of first-grade number knowledge tutoring with contrasting forms of practice. *Journal of Educational Psychology, 105*(1), 58–77. https://doi.org/10.1037/a0030127

Fuchs, L. S., Malone, A. S., Schumacher, R. F., Namkung, J., Hamlett, C. L., Jordan, N. C., Siegler, R. S., Gersten, R., & Changas, P. (2016). Supported self-explaining during fraction intervention. *Journal of Educational Psychology, 108*(4), 493–508. https://doi.org/10.1037/edu0000073

Fuchs, L. S., Powell, S. R., Hamlett, C. L., Fuchs, D., Cirino, P. T., & Fletcher, J. M. (2008). Remediating computational deficits at third grade: A randomized field trial. *Journal of Research on Educational Effectiveness, 1*(1), 2–32. https://doi.org/10.1080/19345740701692449

Fuchs, L. S., Powell, S. R., Seethaler, P. M., Cirino, P. T., Fletcher, J. M., Fuchs, D., & Hamlett, C. L. (2010). The effects of strategic counting instruction, with and without deliberate practice, on number combination skill among students with mathematics difficulties. *Learning and Individual Differences, 20*(2), 89–100. https://doi.org/10.1016/j.lindif.2009.09.003

Fuchs, L. S., Powell, S. R., Seethaler, P. M., Cirino, P. T., Fletcher, J. M., Fuchs, D., Hamlett, C. L., & Zumeta, R. O. (2009). Remediating number combination and word problem deficits among students with mathematics difficulties: A randomized control trial. *Journal of Educational Psychology, 101*(3), 561–576. https://doi.org/10.1037/a0014701

Fuchs, L. S., Schumacher, R. F., Long, J., Namkung, J., Hamlett, C. L., Cirino, P. T., Jordan, N. C., Siegler, R., Gersten, R., & Changas, P. (2013). Improving at-risk learners' understanding of fractions. *Journal of Educational Psychology, 105*(3), 683–700. https://doi.org/10.1037/a0032446

Fuchs, L. S., Schumacher, R. F., Sterba, S. K., Long, J., Namkung, J., Malone, A., Hamlett, C. L., Jordan, N. C., Gersten, R., Siegler, R. S., & Changas, P. (2014). Does working memory moderate the effects of fraction intervention? An aptitude-treatment interaction. *Journal of Educational Psychology, 106*(2), 499–514. https://doi.org/10.1037/a0034341

Fuchs, L. S., Seethaler, P. M., Sterba, S. K., Craddock, C., Fuchs, D., Compton, D. L., Geary, D. C., & Changas, P. (2021). Closing the word-problem achievement gap in first grade: Schema-based word-problem intervention with embedded language comprehension instruction. *Journal of Educational Psychology, 113*(1), 86–103. https://doi.org/10.1037/edu0000467

Fyfe, E. R., McNeil, N. M., Son, J. Y., & Goldstone, R. L. (2014). Concreteness fading in mathematics and science instruction: A systematic review. *Educational Psychology Review, 26*(1), 9–25. https://doi.org/10.1007/s10648-014-9249-3

Gates, A. I. (1917). Recitation as a factor in memorizing. *Archives of Psychology, 6*(40).

Glaser, C., & Brunstein, J. C. (2007). Improving fourth-grade students' composition skills: Effects of strategy instruction and self-regulation procedures. *Journal of Educational Psychology, 99*(2), 297–310. https://doi.org/10.1037/0022-0663.99.2.297

Good, T. L., Slavings, R. L., Harel, K. H., & Emerson, H. (1987). Student passivity: A study of question asking in K–12 classrooms. *Sociology of Education, 60*(3), 181–199. https://doi.org/10.2307/2112275

Goodwin, B., Gibson, T., & Rouleau, K. (2020). *Learning that sticks: A brain-based model for K–12 instructional design and delivery.* ASCD and McREL.

Graham, S., MacArthur, C., & Schwartz, S. (1995). Effects of goal setting and procedural facilitation on the revising behavior and writing performance of students with writing and learning problems. *Journal of Educational Psychology, 87*(2), 230–240. https://doi.org/10.1037/0022-0663.87.2.230

Gruber, M. J., Gelman, B. D., & Ranganath, C. (2014). States of curiosity modulate hippocampus-dependent learning via the dopaminergic circuit. *Neuron, 84*(2), 486–496. https://doi.org/10.1016/j.neuron.2014.08.060

Guthrie, J. T., Wigfield, A., Barbosa, P., Perencevich, K. C., Taboada, A., Davis, M. H., Scafiddi, N. T., & Tonks, S. (2004). Increasing reading comprehension and engagement through concept-oriented reading instruction. *Journal of Educational Psychology, 96*(3), 403–423. https://doi.org/10.1037/0022-0663.96.3.403

Guthrie, J. T., Wigfield, A., Humenick, N. M., Perencevich, K. C., Taboada, A., & Barbosa, P. (2006). Influences of stimulating tasks on reading motivation and comprehension. *The Journal of Educational Research, 99*(4), 232–246. https://doi.org/10.3200/JOER.99.4.232-246

Hollingsworth, J. R., & Ybarra, S. E. (2017). *Explicit direct instruction (EDI): The power of the well-crafted, well-taught lesson.* Corwin Press.

Hulleman, C. S., Godes, O., Hendricks, B. L., & Harackiewicz, J. M. (2010). Enhancing interest and performance with a utility value intervention. *Journal of Educational Psychology, 102*(4), 880–895. https://doi.org/10.1037/a0019506

Hulleman, C. S., & Harackiewicz, J. M. (2009). Promoting interest and performance in high school science classes. *Science, 326*(5958), 1410–1412. https://doi.org/10.1126/science.1177067

Hunter, M. C. (1982). *Mastery teaching.* Corwin Press.

Hyde, T. S., & Jenkins, J. J. (1969). Differential effects of incidental tasks on the organization and recall of a list of highly associated words. *Journal of Experimental Psychology, 82*(3), 472–481. https://doi.org/10.1037/h0028372

Ives, B. (2007). Graphic organizers applied to secondary algebra instruction for students with learning disorders. *Learning Disabilities Research & Practice, 22*(2), 110–118. https://doi.org/10.1111/j.1540-5826.2007.00235.x

Jitendra, A. K., Dupuis, D. N., Rodriguez, M. C., Zaslofsky, A. F., Slater, S., Cozine-Corroy, K., & Church, C. (2013). A randomized controlled trial of the impact of schema-based instruction on mathematical outcomes for third-grade students with mathematics difficulties. *The Elementary School Journal, 114*(2), 252–276. https://doi.org/10.1086/673199

Jitendra, A. K., Star, J. R., Rodriguez, M., Lindell, M., & Someki, F. (2011). Improving students' proportional thinking using schema-based instruction. *Learning and Instruction, 21*(6), 731–745. https://doi.org/10.1016/j.learninstruc.2011.04.002

Jitendra, A. K., Star, J. R., Starosta, K., Leh, J. M., Sood, S., Caskie, G., Hughes, C. L., & Mack, T. R. (2009). Improving seventh grade students' learning of ratio and proportion: The role of schema-based instruction. *Contemporary Educational Psychology, 34*(3), 250–264. https://doi.org/10.1016/j.cedpsych.2009.06.001

Johnson, D. W., & Johnson, R. T. (1999). Making cooperative learning work. *Theory into Practice, 38*(2), 67–73. https://doi.org/10.1080/00405849909543834

Jones, M. G. (1990). Action zone theory, target students and science classroom interactions. *Journal of Research in Science Teaching, 27*(7), 651–660. https://doi.org/10.1002/tea.3660270705

Joyce, B., & Showers, B. (2002). *Student achievement through staff development* (3rd ed.). ASCD.

Justice, L. M., Meier, J., & Walpole, S. (2005). Learning new words from storybooks: An efficacy study with at-risk kindergartners. *Language, Speech & Hearing Services in Schools, 36*(1), 17–32. https://doi.org/10.1044/0161-1461(2005/003)

Kahneman, D. (2011). *Thinking, fast and slow.* Farrar, Straus & Giroux.

Kalyuga, S., Chandler, P., & Sweller, J. (2001). Learner experience and efficiency of instructional guidance. *Educational Psychology, 21*(1), 5–23. https://doi.org/10.1080/01443410124681

Karpicke, J. D., & Blunt, J. R. (2011). Retrieval practice produces more learning than elaborative studying with concept mapping. *Science, 331*(6018), 772–775. https://doi.org/10.1126/science.1199327

Karpicke, J. D., Blunt, J. R., & Smith, M. A. (2016). Retrieval-based learning: Positive effects of retrieval practice in elementary school children. *Frontiers in Psychology, 7*, 350. https://doi.org/10.3389/fpsyg.2016.00350

Karpicke, J. D., & Smith, M. A. (2012). Separate mnemonic effects of retrieval practice and elaborative encoding. *Journal of Memory and Language, 67*(1), 17–29. https://doi.org/10.1016/j.jml.2012.02.004

Keith, T. Z. (1982). Time spent on homework and high school grades: A large-sample path analysis. *Journal of Educational Psychology, 74*(2), 248–253. https://doi.org/10.1037/0022-0663.74.2.248

Kerr, R., & Booth, B. (1978). Specific and varied practice of a motor skill. *Perceptual and Motor Skills, 46*(2), 395–401. https://doi.org/10.1177/003151257804600201

Kim, J. S., Hemphill, L., Troyer, M., Thomson, J. M., Jones, S. M., LaRusso, M. D., & Donovan, S. (2017). Engaging struggling adolescent readers to improve reading skills. *Reading Research Quarterly, 52*(3), 357–382. https://doi.org/10.1002/rrq.171

Kim, J. S., Olson, C. B., Scarcella, R., Kramer, J., Pearson, M., van Dyk, D., Collins, P., & Land, R. E. (2011). A randomized experiment of a cognitive strategies approach to text-based analytical writing for mainstreamed Latino English language learners in grades 6 to 12. *Journal of Research on Educational Effectiveness, 4*(3), 231–263. https://doi.org/10.1080/19345747.2010.523513

King, A. (1991). Effects of training in strategic questioning on children's problem-solving performance. *Journal of Educational Psychology, 83*(3), 307–317. https://doi.org/10.1037/0022-0663.83.3.307

Kirschner, P., Sweller, J., & Clark, R. E. (2006). Why minimal guidance during instruction does not work: An analysis of the failure of constructivist, discovery, problem-based, experiential, and inquiry-based teaching. *Educational Psychologist, 41*(2), 75–86. https://doi.org/10.1207/s15326985ep4102_1

Kluger, A. N., & DeNisi, A. (1996). The effects of feedback interventions on performance: A historical review, a meta-analysis, and a preliminary feedback intervention theory. *Psychological Bulletin, 119*(2), 254.

Kohn, A. (1999). *Punished by rewards: The trouble with gold stars, incentive plans, A's, praise, and other bribes.* HarperOne.

Kramarski, B., & Mevarech, Z. R. (2003). Enhancing mathematical reasoning in the classroom: The effects of cooperative learning and metacognitive training. *American Educational Research Journal, 40*(1), 281–310. https://doi.org/10.3102/00028312040001281

Langer, J. A., & Applebee, A. N. (1987). *How writing shapes thinking: A study of teaching and learning.* (NCTE Research Report No. 22). National Council of Teachers of English.

Larson, L. R., & Lovelace, M. D. (2013). Evaluating the efficacy of questioning strategies in lecture-based classroom environments: Are we asking the right questions? *Journal on Excellence in College Teaching, 24*(1), 105–122.

Lesaux, N. K., Kieffer, M. J., Kelley, J. G., & Harris, J. R. (2014). Effects of academic vocabulary instruction for linguistically diverse adolescents: Evidence from a randomized field trial. *American Educational Research Journal, 51*(6), 1159–1194. https://doi.org/10.3102/0002831214532165

Levitin, D. J. (2015, September 23). *Why it's so hard to pay attention, explained by science.* Fast Company. https://www.fastcompany.com/3051417/why-its-so-hard-to-pay-attention-explained-by-science

Limpo, T., & Alves, R. A. (2014). Implicit theories of writing and their impact on students' response to a SRSD intervention. *British Journal of Educational Psychology, 84*(4), 571–590. https://doi.org/10.1111/bjep.12042

Lipsey, M. W., Puzio, K., Yun, C., Hebert, M. A., Steinka-Fry, K., Cole, M. W., Roberts, M., Anthony, K. S., & Busick, M. D. (2012). *Translating the statistical representation of the effects of education interventions into more readily interpretable forms.* (NCSER 2013-3000). National Center for Special Education Research, Institute of Education Sciences, U.S. Department of Education.

Loewenstein, G. (1994). The psychology of curiosity: A review and reinterpretation. *Psychology Bulletin, 116*(1), 75–98. https://doi.org/10.1037/0033-2909.116.1.75

Lorch, R. F., Jr., Lorch, E. P., Calderhead, W. J., Dunlap, E. E., Hodell, E. C., & Freer, B. D. (2010). Learning the control of variables strategy in higher and lower achieving classrooms: Contributions of explicit instruction and experimentation. *Journal of Educational Psychology, 102*(1), 90–101. https://doi.org/10.1037/a0017972

Lowry, N., & Johnson, D. W. (1981). Effects of controversy on epistemic curiosity, achievement, and attitudes. *Journal of Social Psychology, 115*, 31–43. https://doi.org/10.1080/00224545.1981.9711985

Lynch, S., Taymans, J., Watson, W. A., Ochsendorf, R. J., Pyke, C., & Szesze, M. J. (2007). Effectiveness of a highly rated science curriculum unit for students with disabilities in general education classrooms. *Exceptional Children, 73*(2), 202–223. https://doi.org/10.1177/001440290707300205

Maheady, L., Mallette, B., Harper, G. F., & Sacca, K. (1991). Heads together: A peer-mediated option for improving the academic achievement of heterogeneous learning groups. *Remedial and Special Education, 12*(2), 25–33. https://doi.org/10.1177/074193259101200206

Marin, L. M., & Halpern, D. F. (2011). Pedagogy for developing critical thinking in adolescents: Explicit instruction produces greatest gains. *Thinking Skills and Creativity, 6*(1), 1–13. https://doi.org/10.1016/j.tsc.2010.08.002

Marzano, R. J. (1998). *A theory-based meta-analysis of research on instruction.* Mid-continent Research for Education and Learning (McREL).

Marzano, R. J. (2001). *A new era of school reform: Going where the research takes us.* McREL.

Marzano, R. J., Pickering, D. J., & Pollock, J. E. (2001). *Classroom instruction that works: Research-based strategies for increasing student achievement.* ASCD and McREL.

Mayfield, K. H., & Chase, P. N. (2002). The effects of cumulative practice on mathematics problem solving. *Journal of Applied Behavior Analysis, 35*(2), 105–123. https://doi.org/10.1901/jaba.2002.35-105

McDaniel, M. A., Agarwal, P. K., Huelser, B. J., McDermott, K. B., & Roediger, H. L., III. (2011). Test-enhanced learning in a middle school science classroom: The effects of quiz frequency and placement. *Journal of Educational Psychology, 103*(2), 399–414. https://doi.org/10.1037/a0021782

McDaniel, M. A., Brown, P. C., & Roediger, H. L., III. (2014). *Make it stick: The science of successful learning.* Harvard University Press.

McDaniel, M. A., & Donnelly, C. M. (1996). Learning with analogy and elaborative interrogation. *Journal of Educational Psychology, 88*(3), 508–519. https://doi.org/10.1037/0022-0663.88.3.508

McDermott, K. B., Agarwal, P. K., D'Antonio, L., Roediger, H. L., III, & McDaniel, M. A. (2014). Both multiple-choice and short-answer quizzes enhance later exam performance in middle and high school classes. *Journal of Experimental Psychology: Applied, 20*(1), 3–21. https://doi.org/10.1037/xap0000004

McDougall, D., & Granby, C. (1996). How expectation of questioning method affects undergraduates' preparation for class. *The Journal of Experimental Education, 65*(1), 43–54. https://doi.org/10.1080/00220973.1996.9943462

McKeown, M. G., Crosson, A. C., Moore, D. W., & Beck, I. L. (2018). Word knowledge and comprehension effects of an academic vocabulary intervention for middle school students. *American Educational Research Journal, 55*(3), 572–616. https://doi.org/10.3102/0002831217744181

McNeil, N. M., Fyfe, E. R., Petersen, L. A., Dunwiddie, A. E., & Brletic-Shipley, H. (2011). Benefits of practicing 4 = 2 + 2: Nontraditional problem formats facilitate children's understanding of mathematical equivalence. *Child Development, 82*(5), 1620–1633. https://doi.org/10.1111/j.1467-8624.2011.01622.x

Medina, J. (2008). *Brain rules: 12 principles for surviving and thriving at work, home, and school*. Pear Press.

Merton, K. (1968). The Matthew effect in science. *Science, 159* (3810), 56–63. https://doi.org/10.1126/science.159.3810.56

Midgette, E., Haria, P., & MacArthur, C. (2008). The effects of content and audience awareness goals for revision on the persuasive essays of fifth- and eighth-grade students. *Reading and Writing, 21*(1), 131–151. https://doi.org/10.1007/s11145-007-9067-9

Miller, G. A. (1956). The magical number seven, plus or minus two: Some limits on our capacity for processing information. *Psychological Review, 63*(2), 81–97. https://doi.org/10.1037/h0043158

Morisano, D., Hirsh, J. B., Peterson, J. B., Pihl, R. O., & Shore, B. M. (2010). Setting, elaborating, and reflecting on personal goals improves academic performance. *Journal of Applied Psychology, 95*(2), 255–264. https://doi.org/10.1037/a0018478

Mwangi, W., & Sweller, J. (1998). Learning to solve compare word problems: The effect of example format and generating self-explanations. *Cognition and Instruction, 16*(2), 173–199. https://doi.org/10.1207/s1532690xci1602_2

Nelson, J. R., Vadasy, P. F., & Sanders, E. A. (2011). Efficacy of a Tier 2 supplemental root word vocabulary and decoding intervention with kindergarten Spanish-speaking English learners. *Journal of Literacy Research, 43*(2), 184–211. https://doi.org/10.1177/1086296X11403088

Newell, A., & Simon, H. A. (1972). *Human problem solving*. Prentice-Hall.

Nokes, T. J., Schunn, C. D., & Chi, M. T. H. (2010). Problem solving and human expertise. *International Encyclopedia of Education* (Vol. 5, pp. 265–272). Elsevier. https://doi.org/10.1016/B978-0-08-044894-7.00486-3

Olson, C. B., Kim, J. S., Scarcella, R., Kramer, J., Pearson, M., van Dyk, D. A., Collins, P., & Land, R. E. (2012). Enhancing the interpretive reading and analytical writing of mainstreamed English learners in secondary school: Results from a randomized field trial using a cognitive strategies approach. *American Educational Research Journal, 49*(2), 323–355. https://doi.org/10.3102/0002831212439434

Olson, C. B., & Land, R. (2007). A cognitive strategies approach to reading and writing instruction for English language learners in secondary school. *Research in the Teaching of English, 41*(3), 269–303. https://archive.nwp.org/cs/public/download/nwp_file/8538/Booth_Olson,_Carol,_et_al.pdf?x-r=pcfile_d

Olson, C. B., Matuchniak, T., Chung, H. Q., Stumpf, R., & Farkas, G. (2017). Reducing achievement gaps in academic writing for Latinos and English learners in grades 7–12. *Journal of Educational Psychology, 109*(1), 1–21. https://doi.org/10.1037/edu0000095

Outhwaite, L. A., Faulder, M., Gulliford, A., & Pitchford, N. J. (2019). Raising early achievement in math with interactive apps: A randomized control trial. *Journal of Educational Psychology, 111*(2), 284–298. https://doi.org/10.1037/edu0000286

Page-Voth, V., & Graham, S. (1999). Effects of goal setting and strategy use on the writing performance and self-efficacy of students with writing and learning problems. *Journal of Educational Psychology, 91*(2), 230–240. https://doi.org/10.1037/0022-0663.91.2.230

Paivio, A. (1991). *Images in mind: The evolution of a theory*. Harvester Wheatsheaf.

Pashler, H., McDaniel, M., Rohrer, D., & Bjork, R. (2008). Learning styles: Concepts and evidence. *Psychological Science in the Public Interest, 9*(3), 105–119.

Pearsall, G., & Harris, N. (2019). *Tilting your teaching: Seven simple shifts that can substantially improve student learning*. McREL International.

Peng, P., & Fuchs, D. (2017). A randomized control trial of working memory training with and without strategy instruction: Effects on young children's working memory and comprehension. *Journal of Learning Disabilities, 50*(1), 62–80. https://doi.org/10.1177/0022219415594609

Powell, S. R., Driver, M. K., & Julian, T. E. (2015). The effect of tutoring with nonstandard equations for students with mathematics difficulty. *Journal of Learning Disabilities, 48*(5), 523–534. https://doi.org/10.1177/0022219413512613

Powell, S. R., Fuchs, L. S., Fuchs, D., Cirino, P. T., & Fletcher, J. M. (2009). Effects of fact retrieval tutoring on third-grade students with math difficulties with and without reading difficulties. *Learning Disabilities Research & Practice, 24*(1), 1–11. https://doi.org/10.1111/j.1540-5826.2008.01272.x

Pressley, M., McDaniel, M. A., Turnure, J. E., Wood, E., & Ahmad, M. (1987). Generation and precision of elaboration: Effects on intentional and incidental learning. *Journal of Experimental Psychology: Learning, Memory, and Cognition, 13*(2), 291–300. https://doi.org/10.1037/0278-7393.13.2.291

Pullen, P. C., Tuckwiller, E. D., Konold, T. R., Maynard, K. L., & Coyne, M. D. (2010). A tiered intervention model for early vocabulary instruction: The effects of tiered instruction for young students at risk for reading disability. *Learning Disabilities Research & Practice, 25*(3), 110–123. https://doi.org/10.1111/j.1540-5826.2010.00309.x

Quitadamo, I. J., & Kurtz, M. J. (2007). Learning to improve: Using writing to increase critical thinking performance in general education biology. *CBE—Life Sciences Education, 6*(2), 140–154. https://doi.org/10.1187/cbe.06-11-0203

Rawson, K. A., & Dunlosky, J. (2011). Optimizing schedules of retrieval practice for durable and efficient learning: How much is enough? *Journal of Experimental Psychology: General, 140*(3), 283–302. https://doi.org/10.1037/a0023956

Richardson, M., Abraham, C., & Bond, R. (2012). Psychological correlates of university students' academic performance: A systematic review and meta-analysis. *Psychological Bulletin, 138*(2), 353–387. https://doi.org/10.1037/a0026838

Rittle-Johnson, B., & Star, J. R. (2007). Does comparing solution methods facilitate conceptual and procedural knowledge? An experimental study on learning to solve equations. *Journal of Educational Psychology, 99*(3), 561–574. https://doi.org/10.1037/0022-0663.99.3.561

Roediger, H. L., III, & Pyc, M. A. (2012). Inexpensive techniques to improve education: Applying cognitive psychology to enhance educational practice. *Journal of Applied Research in Memory and Cognition, 1*(4), 242–248. https://doi.org/10.1016/j.jarmac.2012.09.002

Rohrer, D., Dedrick, R. F., & Burgess, K. (2014). The benefit of interleaved mathematics practice is not limited to superficially similar kinds of problems. *Psychonomic Bulletin & Review, 21*(5), 1323–1330. https://doi.org/10.3758/s13423-014-0588-3

Rohrer, D., Dedrick, R. F., Hartwig, M. K., & Cheung, C.-N. (2020). A randomized controlled trial of interleaved mathematics practice. *Journal of Educational Psychology, 112*(1), 40–52. https://doi.org/10.1037/edu0000367

Rohrer, D., & Pashler, H. (2010). Recent research on human learning challenges conventional instructional strategies. *Educational Researcher, 39*(5), 406–412. https://doi.org/10.3102/0013189X10374770

Roschelle, J., Feng, M., Murphy, R. F., & Mason, C. A. (2016). Online mathematics homework increases student achievement. *AERA Open, 2*(4), 1–12. https://doi.org/10.1177/2332858416673968

Roschelle, J., Shechtman, N., Tatar, D., Hegedus, S., Hopkins, B., Empson, S., Knudsen, J., & Gallagher, L. P. (2010). Integration of technology, curriculum, and professional development for advancing middle school mathematics: Three large-scale studies. *American Educational Research Journal, 47*(4), 833–878. https://doi.org/10.3102/0002831210367426

Rowe, M. B. (1986). Wait time: Slowing down may be a way of speeding up! *Journal of Teacher Education, 37*(1), 43–50. https://doi.org/10.1177/002248718603700110

Saddler, B., & Graham, S. (2005). The effects of peer-assisted sentence-combining instruction on the writing performance of more and less skilled young writers. *Journal of Educational Psychology, 97*(1), 43–54. https://doi.org/10.1037 /0022-0663.97.1.43

Sawyer, R., Graham, S., & Harris, K. (1992). Direct teaching, strategy instruction, and strategy instruction with explicit self-regulation: Effects on the composition skills and self-efficacy of students with learning disabilities. *Journal of Educational Psychology, 84*(3), 340–352. https://doi.org/10.1037/0022-0663.84.3.340

Scheiter, K., Gerjets, P., & Schuh, J. (2010). The acquisition of problem-solving skills in mathematics: How animations can aid understanding of structural problem features and solution procedures. *Instructional Science, 38*(5), 487–502. https://doi.org/10.1007/s11251-009-9114-9

Schunk, D. H., & Swartz, C. W. (1991). *Process goals and progress feedback: Effects on children's self-efficacy and skills*. Paper presented at American Educational Research Association Annual Meeting, Chicago. https://files.eric.ed.gov/fulltext /ED330713.pdf

Schunk, D. H., & Swartz, C. W. (1993). Goals and progress feedback: Effects on self-efficacy and writing achievement. *Contemporary Educational Psychology, 18*(3), 337–354. https://doi.org/10.1006/ceps.1993.1024

Schworm, S., & Renkl, A. (2006). Computer-supported example-based learning: When instructional explanations reduce self-explanations. *Computers & Education, 46*(4), 426–445. https://doi.org/10.1016/j.compedu.2004.08.011

Scruggs, T. E., Mastropieri, M. A., & Sullivan, G. S. (1994). Promoting relational thinking: Elaborative interrogation for students with mild disabilities. *Exceptional Children, 60*(5), 450–457. https://doi.org/10.1177/001440299406000507

Seligman, M. E. (2006). *Learned optimism: How to change your mind and your life*. Vintage.

Silverman, R., & Hines, S. (2009). The effects of multimedia-enhanced instruction on the vocabulary of English-language learners and non-English-language learners in pre-kindergarten through second grade. *Journal of Educational Psychology, 101*(2), 305–314. https://doi.org/10.1037/a0014217

Slavin, R. E. (1990). *Cooperative learning: Theory, research and practice*. Prentice Hall.

Smith, B. L., Holliday, W. G., & Austin, H. W. (2010). Students' comprehension of science textbooks using a question-based reading strategy. *Journal of Research in Science Teaching, 47*(4), 363–379. https://doi.org/10.1002/tea.20378

Souza, D. A. (2011). *How the brain learns* (4th ed.). Corwin Press.

Star, J. R., & Rittle-Johnson, B. (2009). It pays to compare: An experimental study on computational estimation. *Journal of Experimental Child Psychology, 102*(4), 408–426. https://doi.org/10.1016/j.jecp.2008.11.004

Stevens, R. J. (2003). Student team reading and writing: A cooperative learning approach to middle school literacy instruction. *Educational Research and Evaluation, 9*(2), 137–160. https://doi.org/10.1076/edre.9.2.137.14212

Swanson, H. L., Lussier, C., & Orosco, M. (2013). Effects of cognitive strategy interventions and cognitive moderators on word problem solving in children at risk for problem solving difficulties. *Learning Disabilities Research & Practice, 28*(4), 170–183. https://doi.org/10.1111/ldrp.12019

Sweller, J. (1988). Cognitive load during problem solving: Effects on learning. *Cognitive Science, 12*(2), 257–285. https://doi.org/10.1016/0364-0213(88)90023-7

Tajika, H., Nakatsu, N., Nozaki, H., Neumann, E., & Maruno, S. (2007). Effects of self-explanation as a metacognitive strategy for solving mathematical word problems. *Japanese Psychological Research, 49*(3), 222–233. https://doi.org/10.1111/j.1468-5884.2007.00349.x

Taylor, K., & Rohrer, D. (2010). The effects of interleaved practice. *Applied Cognitive Psychology, 24*(6), 837–848. https://doi.org/10.1002/acp.1598

Terwel, J., van Oers, B., van Dijk, I., & van den Eeden, P. (2009). Are representations to be provided or generated in primary mathematics education? Effects on transfer. *Educational Research and Evaluation, 15*(1), 25–44. https://doi.org/10.1080/13803610802481265

Tong, F., Irby, B. J., Lara-Alecio, R., Guerrero, C., Fan, Y., & Huerta, M. (2014). A randomized study of a literacy-integrated science intervention for low-socio-economic status middle school students: Findings from first-year implementation. *International Journal of Science Education, 36*(12), 2083–2109. https://doi.org/10.1080/09500693.2014.883107

Tournaki, N. (2003). The differential effects of teaching addition through strategy instruction versus drill and practice to students with and without learning disabilities. *Journal of Learning Disabilities, 36*(5), 449–458. https://doi.org/10.1177/00222194030360050601

Townsend, D., & Collins, P. (2009). Academic vocabulary and middle school English learners: An intervention study. *Reading and Writing, 22*(9), 993–1019. https://doi.org/10.1007/s11145-008-9141-y

Troia, G. A., & Graham, S. (2002). The effectiveness of a highly explicit, teacher-directed strategy instruction routine: Changing the writing performance of students with learning disabilities. *Journal of Learning Disabilities, 35*(4), 290–305. https://doi.org/10.1177/00222194020350040101

University of New South Wales. (2012, November 28). Four is the "magic" number. *ScienceDaily.* https:// www.sciencedaily.com/releases/2012/11/121128093930.htm

Vadasy, P. F., & Sanders, E. A. (2008). Code-oriented instruction for kindergarten students at risk for reading difficulties: A replication and comparison of instructional groupings. *Reading and Writing, 21*(9), 929–963. https://doi.org/10.1007/s11145-008-9119-9

Vadasy, P. F., & Sanders, E. A. (2010). Efficacy of supplemental phonics-based instruction for low-skilled kindergarteners in the context of language minority status and classroom phonics instruction. *Journal of Educational Psychology, 102*(4), 786–803. https://doi.org/10.1037/a0019639

Vadasy, P. F., Sanders, E. A., & Logan Herrera, B. (2015). Efficacy of rich vocabulary instruction in fourth- and fifth-grade classrooms. *Journal of Research on Educational Effectiveness, 8*(3), 325–365. https://doi.org/10.1080/19345747.2014.933495

van Merriënboer, J. J. G., & Sweller, J. (2005). Cognitive load theory and complex learning: Recent developments and future directions. *Educational Psychology Review, 17,* 147–177. https://doi.org/10.1007/s10648-005-3951-0

Vaughn, S., Cirino, P. T., Linan-Thompson, S., Mathes, P. G., Carlson, C. D., Hagan, E. C., Pollard-Durodola, S. D., Fletcher, J. M., & Francis, D. J. (2006). Effectiveness of a Spanish intervention and an English intervention for English-language learners at risk for reading problems. *American Educational Research Journal, 43*(3), 449–487. https://doi.org/10.3102/00028312043003449

Vaughn, S., Martinez, L. R., Wanzek, J., Roberts, G., Swanson, E., & Fall, A.-M. (2017). Improving content knowledge and comprehension for English language learners: Findings from a randomized control trial. *Journal of Educational Psychology, 109*(1), 22–34. https://doi.org/10.1037/edu0000069

Vygotsky, L. S. (1978). *Mind in society*. Harvard University Press.

Walton, G., & Cohen, G. L. (2011). A brief social-belonging intervention improves academic and health outcomes of minority students. *Science, 331*(6023), 1447–1451. https://doi.org/10.1126/science.1198364

Wanzek, J., Vaughn, S., Kent, S. C., Swanson, E. A., Roberts, G., Haynes, M., Fall, A.-M., Stillman-Spisak, S. J., & Solis, M. (2014). The effects of team-based learning on social studies knowledge acquisition in high school. *Journal of Research on Educational Effectiveness, 7*(2), 183–204. https://doi.org/10.1080/19345747.2013.836765

Wasik, B. A., & Bond, M. A. (2001). Beyond the pages of a book: Interactive book reading and language development in preschool classrooms. *Journal of Educational Psychology, 93*(2), 243. https://doi.org/10.1037/0022-0663.93.2.243

Williams, J. P., Nubla-Kung, A. M., Pollini, S., Stafford, K. B., Garcia, A., & Snyder, A. E. (2007). Teaching cause-effect text structure through social studies content to at-risk second graders. *Journal of Learning Disabilities, 40*(2), 111–120. https://doi.org/10.1177/00222194070400020201

Williams, J. P., Pollini, S., Nubla-Kung, A. M., Snyder, A. E., Garcia, A., Ordynans, J. G., & Atkins, J. G. (2014). An intervention to improve comprehension of cause/effect through expository text structure instruction. *Journal of Educational Psychology, 106*(1), 1–17. https://doi.org/10.1037/a0033215

Willingham, D. T. (2003). Students remember what they think about. *American Educator, 27*(2), 37–41.

Willingham, D. T. (2007). Critical thinking: Why it is so hard to teach? *American Educator, 31*, 8–19.

Woloshyn, V. E., Pressley, M., & Schneider, W. (1992). Elaborative-interrogation and prior-knowledge effects on learning of facts. *Journal of Educational Psychology, 84*(1), 115–124. https://doi.org/10.1037/0022-0663.84.1.115

Wong, R. M., Lawson, M. J., & Keeves, J. (2002). The effects of self-explanation training on students' problem solving in high-school mathematics. *Learning and Instruction, 12*(2), 233–262. https://doi.org/10.1016/S0959-4752(01)00027-5

Wood, C., Fitton, L., Petscher, Y., Rodriguez, E., Sunderman, G., & Lim, T. (2018). The effect of e-book vocabulary instruction on Spanish–English speaking children. *Journal of Speech, Language, and Hearing Research, 61*(8), 1945–1969. https://doi.org/10.1044/2018_JSLHR-L-17-0368

Wood, E., & Hewitt, K. L. (1993). Assessing the impact of elaborative strategy instruction relative to spontaneous strategy use in high achievers. *Exceptionality, 4*(2), 65–79. https://doi.org/10.1207/s15327035ex0402_1

Woodward, J. (2006). Developing automaticity in multiplication facts: Integrating strategy instruction with timed practice drills. *Learning Disability Quarterly, 29*(4), 269–289. https://doi.org/10.2307/30035554

Xin, Y. P., Jitendra, A. K., & Deatline-Buchman, A. (2005). Effects of mathematical word problem-solving instruction on middle school students with learning problems. *The Journal of Special Education, 39*(3), 181–192. https://doi.org/10.1177/00224669050390030501

Zhou, N., & Yadav, A. (2017). Effects of multimedia story reading and questioning on preschoolers' vocabulary learning, story comprehension and reading engagement. *Educational Technology Research and Development, 65*(6), 1523–1545. https://doi.org/10.1007/s11423-017-9533-2

Index

The letter *f* following a page number denotes a figure.

About the Authors

Bryan Goodwin is president and CEO of McREL International, a nonprofit school improvement organization that helps school systems worldwide harness the power of student curiosity, the science of learning, and evidence-based teaching practices to support the success of each and every learner. He has written many books that translate research into practice for educators, including *Building a Curious School: Restore the Joy That Brought You to School* (2020), *Learning That Sticks: A Brain-Based Model for K–12 Instructional Design and Delivery* (2020), *Unstuck: How Curiosity, Peer Coaching, and Teaming Can Change Schools* (2018), *Balanced Leadership for Powerful Learning: Tools for Achieving Success in Your School* (2015), *The 12 Touchstones of Good Teaching: A Checklist for Staying Focused Every Day* (2013), and *Simply Better: Doing What Matters Most to Change the Odds for Student Success* (2011). He also writes a regular research column for ASCD's monthly *Educational Leadership* magazine. Goodwin has shared his insights with audiences worldwide. A former classroom teacher and journalist, he holds a BA from Baylor University and an MA from the University of Virginia.

Kristin (Kris) Rouleau, EdD, is the executive director of learning services and innovation at McREL International, working with schools, districts, and state departments of education both domestically and internationally as they navigate change and implement practices and structures to reduce variability and increase student achievement. Through consulting, coaching, and facilitation of professional learning, Rouleau provides services, strategies, and technical assistance to support change efforts, with a particular passion for supporting teacher teams, school and district leaders, and education agencies in their continuous improvement journey. She is also committed to ensuring equitable achievement for all students, strongly believing in the capacity of all students to achieve at high levels and the power of teachers and leaders to positively impact the lives of the students they serve.

As a coauthor of *Learning That Sticks* (2020), *Curiosity Works: A Guidebook for Moving Your School from Improvement to Innovation* (2018), and *Unstuck: How Curiosity, Peer Coaching, and Teaming Can Change Your School* (2018), Rouleau shares responsibility for new product and service development focused on leveraging curiosity to improve teaching, leading, and learning. She is a licensed school administrator with more than 30 years of experience in education, working in a variety of racially and culturally diverse communities. She has served as a classroom teacher, curriculum specialist, elementary school principal, and district-level curriculum administrator. Rouleau earned administrative credentials at the University of Washington and holds an MA in curriculum and teaching from Michigan State University and a BA in elementary education from Western Michigan University. She earned her EdD at the University of Colorado in leadership for educational equity, with a concentration in professional learning and technology.

Cheryl Abla is a senior managing consultant at McREL International, where she develops workshops and professional learning sessions for K–12 teachers on research-based instructional strategies in the areas of instructional technology, English learners, and developing a learner-centered classroom and school environment. She also provides consultation for technology integration, technology leadership, and McREL's classroom observation software, Power Walkthrough®. Prior to joining McREL, Abla taught all grades from 1–12 for more than 20 years. She is a coauthor of *Tools for Classroom Instruction That Works* (2018) and a contributor to the George Lucas Educational Foundation's *Edutopia* blog.

Karen Baptiste, EdD, is a consulting director of learning services and innovation at McREL International, where she provides professional learning and consulting services to schools, districts, and educational agencies. Baptiste's career started in the New York City Department of Education, where she was a special educator, instructional coach, and director of special education. She has worked with K–12 schools across the United States to support improved teaching and learning with an emphasis on quality implementation of evidence-based instructional strategies, including helping teachers create learning environments that encourage student voice and ownership of learning. Her experience also includes being an executive coach to state, district, and school leaders across the nation to transform school culture and educational experiences for students and their families.

Tonia Gibson is a senior managing consultant for McREL International's learning services team. She supports education ministries, district and school leaders, and teachers in using research to improve professional practices and support systemic improvement. She works with educators to address their identified needs, employing a range of strategies including using data for reflection, observations of practice, and analyzing people/organizations performance data. In addition to leading workshops and presenting at conferences, Gibson has developed practical guides and materials for teachers and leaders and coauthored *Unstuck: How Curiosity, Peer Coaching, and Teaming Can Change Your School* (2018). She served as a teacher and assistant principal at primary schools in Melbourne, Australia.

Michele Kimball, a managing consultant at McREL International, leverages her experience as a bilingual early childhood educator in Texas and as a national school support consultant to develop and support educators in ways that have a lasting impact on their students. She has helped educators and educational leaders identify and understand evidence-based best practices, skills, and processes that can be used to change their school culture, support school goals, and advance student learning. Kimball's experience includes providing data-driven, relevant professional learning and coaching services that contribute to building campuswide instructional capacity based on teachers' and students' needs.

About McREL

McREL International is an internationally recognized nonprofit education research and development organization, with offices in Denver, Colorado; Honolulu, Hawai'i; and Cheyenne, Wyoming. Since 1966, McREL has helped translate research and professional wisdom about what works in education into practical guidance for educators. Our expert staff members and affiliates include respected researchers, experienced consultants, and published writers who provide educators with research-based guidance, consultation, and professional development for improving student outcomes.

Related ASCD Resources: Effective Instruction

At the time of publication, the following resources were available (ASCD stock numbers in parentheses):

The 12 Touchstones of Good Teaching: A Checklist for Staying Focused Every Day by Bryan Goodwin and Elizabeth Ross Hubbell (#113009)

Better Learning Through Structured Teaching: A Framework for the Gradual Release of Responsibility, 3rd Edition by Douglas Fisher and Nancy Frey (#121031)

Enhancing Professional Practice: A Framework for Teaching, 2nd Edition by Charlotte Danielson (#106034)

The Instructional Playbook: The Missing Link for Translating Research into Practice by Jim Knight, Ann Hoffman, Michelle Harris, and Sharon Thomas (#122020)

Learning That Sticks: A Brain-Based Model for Instructional Design and Delivery by Bryan Goodwin with Tonia Gibson and Kristin Rouleau (#120032)

Research-Based Instructional Strategies That Work (Quick Reference Guide) by Bryan Goodwin and Kristin Rouleau (#QRG122037)

Simply Better: Doing What Matters Most to Change the Odds for Student Success by Bryan Goodwin (#111038)

Teaching for Deeper Learning: Tools to Engage Students in Meaning Making by Jay McTighe and Harvey F. Silver (#120022)

Unstuck: How Curiosity, Peer Coaching, and Teaming Can Change Your School by Bryan Goodwin, Kristin Rouleau, Dale Lewis, and Tonia Gibson (#118036)

Using Brain Science to Make Learning Stick (Quick Reference Guide) by Bryan Goodwin and Tonia Gibson (#QRG120087)

Why Are We Still Doing That? Positive Alternatives to Problematic Teaching Practices by Pérsida Himmele and William Himmele (#122010)

For up-to-date information about ASCD resources, go to www.ascd.org. You can search the complete archives of *Educational Leadership* at www.ascd.org/el. For more information, send an email to member@ascd.org; call 1-800-933-2723 or 703-578-9600; send a fax to 703-575-5400; or write to Information Services, ASCD, 2800 Shirlington Road, Suite 1001, Arlington, VA 22206 USA

WHOLE CHILD
TENETS

The ASCD Whole Child approach is an effort to transition from a focus on narrowly defined academic achievement to one that promotes the long-term development and success of all children. Through this approach, ASCD supports educators, families, community members, and policymakers as they move from a vision about educating the whole child to sustainable, collaborative actions.

The New Classroom Instruction That Works relates to the **engaged**, **supported**, and **challenged** tenets.

For more about the ASCD Whole Child approach, visit **www.ascd.org/wholechild.**

1 HEALTHY
Each student enters school healthy and learns about and practices a healthy lifestyle.

2 SAFE
Each student learns in an environment that is physically and emotionally safe for students and adults.

3 ENGAGED
Each student is actively engaged in learning and is connected to the school and broader community.

4 SUPPORTED
Each student has access to personalized learning and is supported by qualified, caring adults.

5 CHALLENGED
Each student is challenged academically and prepared for success in college or further study and for employment and participation in a global environment.